D0907473

Overcoming Anxiety and Depression in Teens

Conquer Your Thoughts and Feelings with a Positive Mindset

Richard Bass

Table of Contents

Introduction

It's no secret that societal pressures are on the rise. From mass shootings to a life-threatening pandemic, the younger generations are finding it difficult to cope with mental health issues. Gen Zs—teens and young adults between 15 and 21 years old—are reported to be more stressed than any other generation. They hear about the horrors of our time from social media and news blogs, but feel as though these are matters beyond their control.

In the APA Stress in America survey, 9 out of 10 Gen Z adults reported feeling at least one physical or emotional symptom due to stress. Some of the common symptoms mentioned were depression or sadness (58%) and lacking interest or motivation

(55%) (Bethune, 2019). Only half of those who completed the survey believed they were doing enough to manage their stress.

The stigma surrounding mental health has made it difficult for teens battling to seek professional help. In a 2015 survey on millennials conducted by the American University, 84% of respondents believed that mental health was more of a sensitive topic than other forms of health, and close to 90% of respondents agreed with the statement that young people were "influenced by other people's judgments and opinions when deciding to seek mental health care" (Lorusso & Barnes, 2019).

The only way to end this stigma is by raising awareness about mental health issues affecting teens and young adults and starting discussions around various coping techniques and strategies that can help in managing feelings of stress and anxiety. American singer, songwriter, and Grammy Award winner, Billie Eilish, is seen as an idol to most teens; however, like any other young person, she also battled with depression. During a Grammy TV Special in 2019, she shared her experience grappling with suicidal thoughts and admitted that she never thought she would make it to 17.

But Billie Eilish isn't the only famous teen star who knows what it's like to suffer from mental illness. Justin Bieber, the pop star with over 223 million followers on Instagram and sold-out tours worldwide, has been open about his battle with mental illness. In his YouTube documentary called *Justin Bieber: Next Chapter*, the star shared his experience of having suicidal thoughts. "There was times where I was really, really suicidal," he says, "Like, man, is this pain ever going to go away? It was so consistent, the pain was so consistent. I was just suffering, right? So, I'm just like, man, I would rather not feel this than feel this" (Bieber, 2020).

One common sentiment shared by famous young people who have experienced mental illness is this: You are not alone. Indeed, in the midst of negative thinking, spiraling deeper into a dark place in your mind, it can feel like you are alone. You might even feel embarrassed for having such harmful or mean thoughts. However, what you are experiencing is common and it has a name—mental illness. Learning more about your kind of symptoms or illness can make it easier to cope with the physical and emotional pain that comes with it. You can also better understand the vocabulary used to describe what you are feeling so that you can share your experience with others.

This book is geared toward the Gen Zs who are a group of teens and young adults on the cusp of adulthood; however, parents and educators will find the book informative too. The purpose of this book is to raise awareness about how mental health affects these young people and provide exercises and techniques that can be administered at home or in schools as part of mental health programs.

The book has been designed using Cognitive Behavioral Therapy (CBT) techniques, which are techniques that help people identify and work through negative thoughts, regulate strong emotions, and change destructive behaviors. CBT has been proven successful in treating a range of mental health issues, such as anxiety, depression, anger issues, panic attacks, eating disorders, and phobias. The goal of the techniques presented in this book is to teach young people that even though they cannot control what happens to them or around them, they can control how they interpret events and situations in their environment and how they form their own identities.

Chapter 1:

Anxiety 101

In this chapter, you will learn:

- How to get to grips with anxiety (the types and symptoms of anxiety).

- The various causes of anxiety.

- Different treatment options and whether anxiety can be healed for good.

Are You Nervous or Anxious?

Have you ever heard someone say, "This is giving me so much anxiety!" when in fact, the situation was making them feel nervous? It's common for nervousness to be confused with anxiety, and perhaps we should distinguish between the two before we carry on.

Nervousness is a natural reaction you feel when you are placed in a challenging situation. You might be sitting in the exam room or standing up in front of an auditorium of people, and suddenly feel nervous. There are a few physical sensations that can accompany your feelings of nervousness, like having sweaty palms, feeling light-headed, or having a racing heartbeat.

Nervousness can at times also make you doubt your abilities to perform well at a task. When you feel nervous around new people, for example, you might get shy and find it difficult to strike up a conversation. However, once you have warmed up to them and your nervous feelings are gone, you are able to be yourself around them. Nervousness tends to go away after you have calmed yourself down or completed the challenging task that made you feel uncomfortable. When faced with the same task in the future, you may show more confidence in performing it because it doesn't frighten you anymore.

In contrast, anxiety is an ongoing feeling of fear and dread that you experience, even when you are not exposed to a threatening situation. On a physical level, it can feel like your body is ready to fight or escape possible danger. The danger doesn't need to be real for it to feel real—even imagined negative thoughts are enough to make you feel stressed.

The symptoms of anxiety are similar to the symptoms of nervousness; however, the difference is that with anxiety these feelings appear on a regular basis. For example, you might wake up with a racing heartbeat which can make you feel on edge.

This feeling can continue throughout the day, being worsened by small triggers like being late for school or work.

Moreover, the feeling of dread that is usually a symptom of an anxiety disorder can make you avoid certain social settings that make you feel uncomfortable. For example, if you have a social anxiety disorder, everyday social interactions with people cause excessive fear, and to avoid feeling this way, you might decide to avoid crowds of people, busy locations, or being placed in a situation where you need to engage in conversation with others.

There are a few practical ways to determine if what you are feeling is nervousness or anxiety:

1. How Long Does Your Feeling Last?

In general, nervousness ends as soon as the challenging task, or what you consider an embarrassing situation, is over. You might even look back at your experience and wonder why you were so afraid. On the other hand, anxiety is a state of fear that persists regardless of the context; however, it can heighten or feel less noticeable when you are around certain people or environments.

2. How Intense Is Your Feeling?

Nervousness feels uncomfortable, although it won't stop you from going ahead and performing the challenging task. You might dread every minute of it, but you're open to doing it anyway. Anxiety heightens the threat level of a task or situation to the extent that you don't feel safe performing the task or being in that situation. Therefore, rather than continuing with the task, your natural instinct is to physically remove yourself or emotionally withdraw.

3. Where Does Your Feeling Come From?

You can generally pinpoint the specific task or situation that is making you nervous. It could be public speaking, writing a test, playing sports, or meeting new people. Each time you are placed in these situations, you can anticipate feeling nervous. However, with anxiety, it isn't always clear what is causing you to feel a sense of fear or panic. You might notice a shortness of breath or sweaty palms, but you aren't sure what exactly is making you feel this way. Remember that since the perceived danger doesn't need to be real to feel real, sometimes your anxiety can be caused by unseen factors, such as overthinking or thinking critical thoughts about yourself.

Types of Anxiety Disorders

It's important to note that having anxiety, or being an anxious person, is not a bad thing. You are not a bad person and your experience is natural. Even if your fears may sometimes be irrational (meaning you are afraid of something that most likely won't cause you harm or most likely won't happen), it doesn't make you an irrational person.

Anxiety is an emotion you get in response to stress, trauma, uncertainty, or feeling easily overwhelmed by life. This feeling can come and go, but it can also become an everyday occurrence depending on your personality, lifestyle, and environment. When you feel anxious on a consistent basis and your anxiety starts getting in the way of your school, relationships, or lifestyle, you can be diagnosed with an anxiety disorder.

Anxiety disorders are the most common type of mental illness in the United States. According to the Anxiety and Depression Association of America (ADAA), 40 million adults in the U.S. who are 18 years and older (18.1% of the population) suffer from an anxiety disorder (Anxiety and Depression Association of America, 2021).

An anxiety disorder isn't something you can diagnose yourself with. If you are experiencing symptoms of an anxiety disorder, the next step is to consult with a licensed physician or mental health specialist who can perform a psychological evaluation on you. During the psychological evaluation, the doctor will ask you several questions about your symptoms, history (or family's history) of mental illness, and whether you are taking any medication. The doctor may ask whether you have been diagnosed with any other psychological conditions in the past, like ADHD, OCD, depression, or an eating disorder. These questions may feel intrusive; however, the purpose is to get a good glimpse of your overall mental health and possible triggers of your anxiety.

There are six main types or classifications of anxiety disorders. These types are the following:

1. Generalized Anxiety Disorder

Generalized Anxiety Disorder (GAD) is characterized by excessive worry or fear that is felt on most days and continues for at least a period of six months. Excessive worry is often related to everyday things like being overwhelmed by household chores, family conflict, or looming deadlines. Common symptoms of GAD include:

- Feeling on edge

- Having difficulties concentrating on tasks

- Being irritable

- Having trouble sleeping

- Experiencing body aches

2. Panic Disorder

Panic disorder is often diagnosed when an individual experiences recurring panic attacks. A panic attack is a sudden feeling of intense fear or nervousness that starts and ends within a few minutes. Some panic attacks can be random in nature, but others are triggered by overwhelming life situations. When triggered, a panic attack can feel like the beginning stages of a heart attack or other life-threatening condition. It's important to seek medical attention when your symptoms continue for a prolonged period of time and come in waves. Common symptoms of panic disorder include:

- Heart palpitations

- Trembling

- Having shortness of breath

- Feeling light-headed

- Nausea or abdominal pain

3. Phobia Disorders

Phobia disorders is a blanket term to describe the fear an individual might have of a range of objects, situations, or activities. In many cases, these fears are irrational but feel real nonetheless. A person can feel extremely endangered by an object or situation that they make every effort to avoid that object or situation. Examples of specific phobias include:

- Fear of heights

- Fear of elevators

- Fear of different kinds of insects or animals

- Fear of going to the dentist

4. Social Anxiety Disorder

Previously called social phobia, social anxiety disorder is the anxiety triggered by being humiliated, rejected, or judged by others in social interactions. An individual with a social anxiety disorder will either try to avoid certain social contexts, like being the center of attention or having to stand up in front of a crowd and speak or endure them with a great amount of discomfort. Common examples of social anxiety disorder are

- Fear of public speaking

- Fear of meeting new people

- Being uncomfortable eating in front of other people

- Being uncomfortable making eye contact with people

- Fear of dating

5. Separation Anxiety

Separation anxiety is the excessive worry or fear about being separated from loved ones. The difference between separation anxiety and the normal feeling of sadness when a loved one departs is that the feeling an individual gets when experiencing separation anxiety is disproportionate to their age, can persist for months (lasts up to four weeks for children and six months for adults), and interferes with daily life. Separation anxiety can also manifest as the fear of the thought of losing a loved one through unexpected death, deportment, or migration. As such, it can create an unhealthy attachment to the person one fears losing.

There are several risk factors that can make you more susceptible to being diagnosed with an anxiety disorder. For instance, if you have temperamental traits like shyness or being a natural worrier, being exposed to stressful life events or a stressful home environment can trigger an anxiety disorder. Additionally, if you have been diagnosed with another type of mental illness like depression or bipolar disorder, or perhaps suffer from physical health conditions like asthma or thyroid problems, it can also make you more vulnerable to experiencing an anxiety disorder. However, only a licensed physician or mental health specialist can offer you an accurate diagnosis.

The Triggers of Anxiety

If anxiety disorders are so common, can you imagine the number of things that can trigger anxiety? In fact, in most cases, it isn't a single factor that causes anxiety, but a combination of factors that eventually cause you to feel overwhelmed. For example, your anxiety could be caused by a combination of your genetics, personality traits, childhood upbringing, and substance abuse.

It's also possible that some events in your life trigger anxiety, while others worsen your feelings of anxiety. Here's a general scenario: You grow up being bullied at secondary school and this causes you to have social anxiety. However, having difficulty making friends in high school can worsen your feelings of social anxiety and cause you to withdraw from your peers even more.

Here's another scenario: As a child, you were extremely attached to your parents and would often cry when dropped off at kindergarten or left with other people. This experience traumatized you and caused you to have separation anxiety. The older you grew, the harder it got to separate yourself from your parents. As a result, when you had to leave home for university, your separation anxiety worsened and even led you to feel depressed.

When it comes to triggers, you can't make them disappear. However, increasing your ability to recognize your triggers can make it easier to cope with them. While there are countless types of triggers, here are five common triggers that can cause anxiety:

1. Health Issues

Suffering from a chronic illness or having a close family member who is suffering from a chronic illness can be stressful, and in some cases lead to anxiety. The fears of receiving an alarming diagnosis or not being able to carry out your everyday routine can make you worry about your health issues. Speaking to your doctor and asking questions about your condition or your loved one's condition can reduce your feelings of anxiety and help you manage your emotions.

2. Caffeine

Caffeine is a natural stimulant found in beverages like tea, coffee, and energy drinks. As a stimulant, it wakes up your central nervous system and makes you feel alert and focused. However, this feeling of alertness can also trigger heart palpitations, headaches, jitters, and an upset stomach. If you are vulnerable to stress and anxiety, drinking caffeinated drinks can worsen your symptoms and make you feel tired, anxious, and agitated.

3. Skipping Meals

When you skip meals your blood sugar levels drop, which can make you feel weak, jittery, and anxious. Eating three balanced meals a day is the best way to maintain your blood sugar levels and ensure you have the energy to last a full day. If you are busy between tasks and can't sit down to have a meal, eating a healthy snack can raise your blood sugar and protect you from fatigue and mood swings.

4. Negative Thinking

The quality of your thoughts, particularly negative thoughts, can also trigger anxiety. What you say to yourself can have a profound effect on your mood, self-esteem, and attitude toward life. Reminding yourself of your flaws and limitations can cause stress and anxiety, and make your fears (whether rational or irrational) seem bigger than what they really are. Changing your language and general beliefs about yourself can improve your self-esteem and empower you to take more risks, step outside of your comfort zone, and live a fulfilling life.

5. Pressure From Your Environment

Sometimes, your stress isn't caused by how you perceive the world, but by the high expectations imposed on you by others. You might feel a lot of pressure to perform well at school, follow a career path chosen by your parents, or live up to your family's ethics and standards. You may also live in an environment that has caused you to grow up quickly and assume what many would consider adult responsibilities. For example, if you have a mentally ill parent, you could be assigned the role of paying bills, cooking and cleaning, as well as looking after your younger siblings. The added responsibility, on top of not being allowed to simply be a kid, can feel overwhelming and lead to anxiety.

There are also practical ways to learn how to identify your triggers. Perhaps the best way is to speak to a counselor or mental health professional who can teach you how to recognize your triggers and how to manage them. If that's not possible, you can take up a fun habit like journaling. Journaling is a practice that will be referred to often throughout the book due to how effective it is in helping you track and work through your thoughts and emotions. All it takes to start journaling is a pen, notebook, and at least 15 minutes of your time. You can use your journal to draw mind maps of how you are feeling, document an incident that you can't get out of your mind, or answer questions about how you are feeling.

When using journaling to identify your triggers, you can bring up emotions that could've been suppressed for many years. This is a positive thing because it means that you can finally recognize how deep-rooted your triggers are and slowly work toward being more comfortable with them. The best way to deal with your triggers isn't to avoid them, but to accept them as important cues or messages that alert you of situations that feel threatening.

Exercise: Journaling 101

Below is a simple journaling exercise to get you familiar with the practice of journaling. The exercise is based on confronting your feelings of worry. You can answer these questions in your journal and provide short or long responses. No one else will read your journal beside you, so feel free to think deeply about the questions and give honest answers.

1. Is there anything you are worried about right now?

2. What are some clues that what you are worried about won't come true?

3. If your worry does not come true, what will happen instead?

4. If your worry does come true, how will you handle it?

5. What do you need to remind yourself right now that can help you cope with your feeling of worry?

6. What habit or action can you take right now that will help you cope with your feeling of worry?

Can Anxiety Be Treated?

A common question that people ask is whether anxiety is curable. The answer to this question is no, but not for reasons you might think. Since anxiety isn't a disease, but rather a natural response to stress, it cannot be completely cured.

Nevertheless, it can be managed so that it no longer interferes with your everyday life. So, what are your options? Here are two common types of treatment that can help you manage your anxiety:

1. Psychotherapy

Anxiety often causes you to become overwhelmed with your emotions. In response to these emotions, you can react negatively by avoiding situations that make you anxious, turning to self-harming behaviors, or thinking negatively about yourself or others. Psychotherapy refers to talking to a mental health practitioner or psychologist about your experiences dealing with anxiety, so they can teach you effective tools on how to cope when you are feeling overwhelmed. In order for these tools to work, you must commit to practicing them regularly, especially when you sense a sudden bout of anxiety arising within you.

A common tool that psychologists use and teach their patients is cognitive-behavioral therapy (CBT). This tool can help patients recognize and label their emotions, catch negative patterns of thinking, and learn ways to calm their minds and body during a trigger. After a while, CBT can reduce the frequency of undesirable thoughts and behaviors and increase the patient's confidence in enduring challenging situations.

2. Medication

If psychotherapy doesn't help you, your doctor may prescribe medication. There are several classifications of medication to treat anxiety, each designed to combat certain symptoms. It's important to discuss the options available to you, the side effects of each medicine, and the treatment plan suitable for you. You should also schedule regular check-ups with your doctor so you can adjust your dosage or try a different kind of medication if the one you are on isn't treating your symptoms.

Self-Assessment Anxiety Quiz

Anxiety is often characterized by symptoms that persist on an ongoing basis. The GAD-7 self-assessment created by Dr. Robert L. Spitzer can help you understand how much your anxiety interferes with your daily life (Spitzer, n.d.). Complete the answers to the short quiz below to determine the severity of your anxiety. Please note that a self-assessment is not a diagnostic tool. You are still encouraged to consult with a specialist to get the proper treatment for your anxiety.

Instructions:

Below are seven questions that ask you about how often you have experienced specific emotions within the past two weeks. Each question is worth a certain amount of points, such as:

Not at all = 0 points

Several days = 1 point

More than half the days = 2 points

Nearly every day = 3 points

When you have answered all of the questions, tally up your score and see your results.

Questions:

1. **Feeling nervous or on edge?**

    a. Not at all

    b. Several days

    c. More than half the days

    d. Nearly every day

2. **Having trouble controlling worrying thoughts?**

    a. Not at all

    b. Several days

    c. More than half the days

    d. Nearly every day

3. **Worrying too much about different situations?**

    a. Not at all

    b. Several days

    c. More than half the days

    d. Nearly every day

4. **Having trouble relaxing?**

    a. Not at all

    b. Several days

   c. More than half the days

   d. Nearly every day

5. Finding it difficult to sit still due to feeling restless?

   a. Not at all

   b. Several days

   c. More than half the days

   d. Nearly every day

6. Becoming easily annoyed or irritable?

   a. Not at all

   b. Several days

   c. More than half the days

   d. Nearly every day

7. Feeling as though something terrible is going to happen?

   a. Not at all

   b. Several days

   c. More than half the days

   d. Nearly every day

Results:

0—4 points: No Anxiety Disorder

You do not report having limitations due to your symptoms of anxiety.

5—8 points: Mild Anxiety Disorder

You report having "somewhat" difficulty performing daily tasks due to your symptoms of anxiety.

9—12 points: Moderate Anxiety Disorder

You report having a very difficult time performing daily tasks due to your symptoms of anxiety.

13 and beyond: Severe Anxiety Disorder

You report having an extremely difficult time performing daily tasks due to your symptoms of anxiety.

Key Takeaways

It's normal to go about your day feeling nervous to perform challenging tasks. However, when these nervous feelings persist for an extended period of time, they may be a sign of an anxiety disorder. Since anxiety is a natural response to stress, it cannot be completely cured. However, through practicing various psychological tools like journaling or CBT, or even going the medication route, you can learn how to manage your feelings of anxiety better. Now that you have an understanding of anxiety, the next step is to learn more about one of the common triggers of anxiety—depression.

Chapter 2:

Depression 101

In this chapter, you will learn:

- What depression is and what actually causes it.

- The types of depression and diagnosis.

- Different treatment options to manage depression.

Can Anybody Be Depressed?

American singer, actress, and songwriter, Demi Lovato, has been open about her battles with mental illness, particularly with her fight with depression and bipolar disorder. She admitted in an interview that she has been battling mental health problems since she was seven years old. Fortunately, she is on her recovery journey and has tried several different kinds of treatment, including psychotherapy, taking medication, and even going to rehab.

But what would make a global superstar like Demi Lovato feel depressed? I mean, from the outside, it seems like jet-setting celebrities have it all. The truth is that mental illness can affect anybody, regardless of your culture, social status, educational background, or lifestyle. What makes a person struggle with mental illness are the kinds of stressors, traumas, and triggers they are exposed to, and the way in which they cope with these factors.

Demi Lovato has openly stated that her mental health battles stem from her attempt to achieve perfection with her image and body. To do this, she would control what she ate, which led to an eating disorder. However, she reached a point where she realized that her search for perfection was making her depressed and wasn't at all as important as she thought."When I realized that perfection is unachievable, no matter who you are, you could literally be the most perfect-looking person on the planet, but there will still be something scientifically imperfect with you" she said, "I just started looking at the years where I was younger and thinking, 'Wow, I wasted so much time stressing about things that don't matter. And I wish I could get that time back'" (Fox, 2020).

Demi Lovato isn't the only young and famous celebrity who has battled with their self-image. Selena Gomez, an American singer, and actress has also been vocal about her struggles with anxiety and depression. When Selena describes how it feels like to live with depression, she said, "My highs were really high, and my lows would take me out for weeks at a time" (Blasberg, 2020). She also mentioned how relieved she was when she received a diagnosis because it meant that she could focus on getting the medical attention she needed, which included therapy, medication, and spending time in treatment facilities.

One of the major factors that contributed to her depression was her addiction to social media. Selena Gomez was the first person in the world to climb all the way to 100 million followers on Instagram. But being the most followed person came with its drawbacks. "As soon as I became the most followed person on Instagram, I sort of freaked out" she told Vogue, "I was an addict, and it felt like I was seeing things I didn't want to see, like it was putting things in my head that I didn't want to care about. I always end up feeling like shit when I look at Instagram" (Haskell, 2017). To manage her depression, Selena has gotten into the habit of taking regular breaks from social media, leaning on her strong support network, and continuing taking her medication and attending therapy.

What Is Depression?

Both Demi Lovato and Selena Gomez have struggled with a mental illness called depression. Depression can be defined as a mental illness that negatively affects how you see yourself, how you feel, and the way you think and act. When unaddressed, depression can cause physical and emotional problems that interfere with the way you work, study, and interact with others.

According to recent stats, 2.5 million young people in the U.S. live with severe depression (depression that interferes with their daily life), and out of that number, over 60% have not received treatment (Mental Health America, 2022). Treating depression requires you to recognize the symptoms first, but this can be difficult when your depressive moods occur during episodes. In other words, you could be feeling upbeat and healthy, then all of a sudden experience an episode of depression that lasts for a few days. After the episode, you may return to your usual upbeat personality, as though nothing happened.

Even though you cannot predict when the next episode will be, the symptoms of depression are almost always the same during each episode. These symptoms may include:

- Sadness

- Fatigue

- Being tearful

- Numbness or hopelessness

- Loss of interest in daily activities

- Insomnia or interrupted sleep

- Self-blame and feelings of worthlessness

- Loss of appetite

- Trouble concentrating

- Body aches and pains

- Recurring thoughts of suicide or death

As seen in Selena's case, it's not unusual for someone to suffer from an anxiety disorder and depression at the same time. In fact, being diagnosed with one type of mental illness can make you more susceptible to another. For example, having recurring thoughts of death can cause someone with depression to experience panic attacks and fear the possibility of dying or something tragic happening to a loved one. However, it works the other way too: Someone with an anxiety disorder can become depressed after several years of living in fear and not having control of their thoughts.

Common Causes of Depression

Have you ever wondered what causes depression? Perhaps you have read about people who seemed to be happy on the outside, but internally were battling severe depression. How does this happen? What factors could lead to someone being diagnosed as depressed? Depression is a complex mental illness that isn't caused by a single factor. There are many reasons someone would become depressed. Some of those reasons include

1. Stressful Life Situations

It's common for negative life circumstances to get you down or cause you to feel anxious. When these feelings persist, you may start to think negatively about yourself or your life. As a response to these negative thoughts, you could start to pull away from your friends, become emotionally numb, or use drugs or social media as an outlet to escape.

2. Personality

Some personality types are more vulnerable to depression. For instance, if you are naturally shy and don't readily express what you are feeling, you can suppress your emotions and try to deal with stress on your own. Not only does this put a lot of pressure on you to work through what you are feeling, but it can also make you feel lonely and depressed. Another example is if you are naturally a high-achiever. You can set standards for your life that are so high that they actually cause you to feel inadequate. When these feelings of inadequacy become negative beliefs you hold about yourself, it can eventually lead to depression.

3. History of Mental Illness

Another way you might be exposed to depression is if there are people in your family who have battled with depression in the past. This usually means that you are genetically predisposed to experiencing depression at some point or another in your life.

However, with the right psychological coping kit, you can beat the odds.

4. Alcohol and Drug Use

Alcohol and drugs are not a direct cause of depression; however, if you are dealing with a lot of stress in your life or you have a personality that makes you vulnerable to becoming depressed, then taking depressants like alcohol, opioids, Benzodiazepines, or sleeping pills can leave you feeling anxious and depressed when the chemicals wear off. Regular cannabis use has also been found to increase the risk of anxiety and depression, although other symptoms you may experience include paranoia or psychosis.

5. Physical Illness

If you have a chronic illness, you may have an increased risk of becoming depressed. It can be triggered by constantly feeling fatigued, being highly medicated, or feeling anxious or hopeless about your health condition.

Types of Depression and Diagnosis

Similar to anxiety, you will need to visit a mental health specialist to receive a diagnosis of depression. The mental health specialist, who may be a psychiatrist, will conduct a psychiatric evaluation. During this evaluation, you may be asked questions about your physical and emotional symptoms, how long they have persisted, and how they have interfered with your daily life. These questions will help the doctor assess the severity of your mental illness.

Afterward, they may diagnose you with a certain classification of depression. Since depression symptoms vary from one person to another, doctors use specifiers to better understand the features of each patient's depression. Here are a few specifiers commonly used:

- **Anxiously distressed:** Depression that comes with a feeling of restlessness or worries about unexpected loss or tragedy in the future.

- **Mixed features:** Depression that comes with mania and includes increased energy, an exaggerated sense of self-importance, and talking too much.

- **Melancholic features:** A severe depression that causes a lack of interest, or indifference, to things that used to bring you pleasure.

- **Atypical features:** Depression that sometimes comes with a burst of positive energy, temporarily feeling excited about an event or situation. Other atypical features may include an increased appetite and being sensitive to rejection.

- **Psychotic features:** Depression that comes with delusions or hallucinations, which may cause you to have negative perceptions about yourself or others.

- **Seasonal pattern:** Depression that often comes with a change of season and less exposure to natural sunlight.

When evaluating you, the doctor may find that your depression is actually a symptom of another related disorder. Here are other mental disorders that often have the same symptoms as depression:

- **Bipolar disorders:** Bipolar disorders refer to a group of mood disorders that cause you to experience frequent mood swings that range from high (manic behavior) to low (depressed behavior).

- **Cyclothymic disorder:** A mood disorder that has symptoms milder than bipolar disorders.

- **Disruptive mood dysregulation disorder:** Another mood disorder that causes chronic feelings of irritability and anger, and can lead to regular emotional outbursts. Although this disorder is usually diagnosed in young children, it can lead to anxiety and depression during adolescence or adulthood.

- **Persistent depressive disorder:** Even though this type of depression isn't disabling, it is chronic and can make it difficult for you to perform your daily tasks and routines.

- **Premenstrual dysphoric disorder:** Depression symptoms that are brought about due to hormonal changes that begin a week before a menstrual period. In most cases, these symptoms are less intense during the onset of a menstrual period and disappear when the period is over.

Treatment Options for Depression

Similar to anxiety disorders, there is no cure for depression; however, there are a variety of treatment options that can help you manage your depression symptoms. Medication and psychotherapy are the two most effective treatments for depression. If you suffer from severe depression, then you may also benefit from hospitalization or attending an outpatient treatment program at a mental health facility.

There are a few antidepressants available to you. Consult with your doctor to find the right medication and dosage for your specific symptoms. During your consultation, discuss any side effects that each medication may come with so you know what to expect.

If taking antidepressants doesn't work for you, you can consider psychotherapy. Psychotherapy encourages you to speak about your experiences with depression to a licensed psychologist who can teach you various coping skills that you can apply in your everyday life. Different kinds of therapies, such as CBT or interpersonal therapy, can be effective in treating depression on a long-term basis.

Psychotherapy doesn't promise to make your depression symptoms go away, but it does promise to develop you into the kind of person who can control their depression symptoms. After regular sessions of psychotherapy, you will be able to:

- Adjust to difficult circumstances in your life.

- Identify negative beliefs that cause you to feel discouraged about your life.

- Explore how your relationships with others affect your mental health and adopt positive habits that can make you feel safe during interactions.

- Identify harmful coping behaviors that worsen your experience with depression and replace them with healthy behaviors.

- Develop the ability to remain resilient during tough times and reframe how you perceive negative situations.

Besides taking medication or psychotherapy, making a few lifestyle adjustments can also help you manage your depression better. Here are some lifestyle tips to consider:

- **Incorporate physical exercise into your day.** Physical exercise can increase the production of endorphins in your body, which are hormones that trigger positive moods and feelings. A little exercise goes a long way! Aim for at least 30 minutes of exercise 3-5 times per week.

- **Avoid drug and alcohol use if you suspect you are feeling depressed.** Depressants such as drugs and alcohol should be avoided when you suspect that your mental health is not good. Instead of making you feel better, they can make your anxiety or depression worse. You can challenge yourself to find healthier and sober ways to have fun, relieve stress, and socialize with your friends.

- **Learn how to set clear and firm boundaries.** Healthy boundaries can ensure you feel safe during interactions with others. Practice saying words like "No", "Not today," or "I didn't appreciate that" so that you can avoid feeling overwhelmed by your relationships.

- **Prioritize self-care.** Practicing self-care is about doing things that improve your physical, mental, and emotional well-being. It could be as simple as tweaking your diet so that you eat healthier foods or making time to journal in your diary or catching up with close friends. Create a list of the activities that make you feel better about yourself, and carry out at least one activity each day.

Self-Assessment Depression Quiz

Not all experiences of depression are the same. Depending on the severity, depression can affect people in different ways. Complete the answers to the short quiz below to determine the severity of your depression. Please note that a self-assessment is not a diagnostic tool. You are still encouraged to consult with a specialist to get the proper treatment for your depression.

Instructions:

Below are nine questions that ask you about how often you have experienced specific depression symptoms within the past two weeks. Each question is worth a certain amount of points, such as:

Not at all = 0 points

Several days = 1 point

More than half the days = 2 points

Nearly every day = 3 points

When you have answered all of the questions, tally up your score and see your results.

Questions:

1. **Feeling depressed or irritable?**

    a. Not at all

    b. Several days

    c. More than half the days

    d. Nearly every day

2. **Little interest in doing the things you once found pleasurable?**

    a. Not at all

    b. Several days

    c. More than half the days

    d. Nearly every day

3. **Loss of appetite, unexplained weight loss or weight gain, overeating?**

    a. Not at all

b. Several days

c. More than half the days

d. Nearly every day

4. **Trouble falling asleep at night or sleeping too much?**

a. Not at all

b. Several days

c. More than half the days

d. Nearly every day

5. **Feeling tired throughout the day, even after getting sufficient sleep?**

a. Not at all

b. Several days

c. More than half the days

d. Nearly every day

6. **Having thoughts of personal inadequacy, thinking that you are not good enough?**

a. Not at all

b. Several days

c. More than half the days

d. Nearly every day

7. **Having difficulty concentrating on work, reading, or watching TV?**

   a. Not at all

   b. Several days

   c. More than half the days

   d. Nearly every day

8. **Moving or speaking slowly, or being fidgety and restless?**

   a. Not at all

   b. Several days

   c. More than half the days

   d. Nearly every day

9. **Thoughts of hurting yourself in some way?**

   a. Not at all

   b. Several days

   c. More than half the days

   d. Nearly every day

Results:

0—4 points: No or Minimal Depression

You do not report having limitations due to your symptoms of depression.

5—9 points: Mild Depression

You report having "somewhat" difficulty performing daily tasks due to your symptoms of depression.

10—14 points: Moderate Depression

You report having a very difficult time performing daily tasks due to your symptoms of depression.

15 and beyond: Severe Depression

You report having an extremely difficult time performing daily tasks due to your symptoms of depression.

Key Takeaways

Depression can affect anybody, despite their social, cultural, or economic background. One of the causes of depression is stressful life events, although having a certain personality trait or a history of mental illness in your family can increase your risk of becoming depressed during stressful times in your life. Fortunately, depression can be treated by taking medication or psychotherapy. While depression cannot be completely cured, you can develop the skills to cope with your symptoms so that they don't interfere with your daily life. The first step in coping with symptoms of anxiety and depression is learning about your avoidance and safety behaviors.

Chapter 3:

Figuring Out Your Avoidance and Safety Behaviors to Overcome Anxiety

In this chapter, you will learn:

- Different avoidance and safety behaviors.

- How to map out your own behaviors so you can avoid your triggers.

What Are Avoidance and Safety Behaviors?

Take a few minutes and think about your go-to behaviors when you are feeling stressed or anxious. What is the first thing you usually do? For many people, their initial reaction is to block out or avoid the triggering situation. In psychology, behaviors that seek to avoid, block, or retreat from stressful situations are known as avoidance behaviors. Instead of helping you cope or face the situation, avoidance behaviors create enough distance so you don't need to deal with it.

When you are under a lot of stress or pressure, getting as far away as possible from a triggering situation seems like the best thing to do. When it is out of your sight or mind, it can feel like it's disappeared. But has it really? Or have you just temporarily pushed it aside? The truth is that avoidance behaviors don't solve a crisis or problem, they only brush it aside so that you don't have to think about it at the moment. Eventually, the crisis or problem creeps up again, and the cycle of avoidance continues.

An example of avoidant behavior could be avoiding medical doctors because you had a bad experience with one and vowed to never consult with a doctor again. Another example is disengaging from a conversation when certain emotional topics are brought up. You could also avoid eating certain foods because you are afraid of what will happen when you eat them (eg. Avoiding carbohydrates because you believe they will make you put on weight).

Another reaction to stress or anxiety is to turn to safety behaviors. Safety behaviors are the precautionary measures you put in place to deal with stressful situations. These behaviors usually stem from childhood, when you felt afraid, lonely, or misunderstood and resorted to certain behaviors that made you feel comforted. For example, if you were a shy kid growing up, you probably took the back seat in the classroom to avoid having to interact with your classmates during the lesson. Or if you were often criticized as a child, you may develop a habit of over-preparing for tests or presentations so that you don't expose yourself to harsh criticism.

Just because safety behaviors have the name "safe" in them, doesn't make them healthy. In fact, psychologists believe that safety behaviors are the milder version of avoidance behaviors. This is because even though you are still engaging in what is perceived as a stressful situation, you haven't fully let go of your fears.

Both avoidance and safety behaviors can give you relief in the short-term, but won't help you confront and cope with stress and anxiety in the long term. The more you avoid dealing with certain situations, the harder it becomes to manage your stress levels. Furthermore, when your list of people, places, and things to avoid increases, your quality of life decreases and you find yourself trapped in a web of fear, unable to explore everything that life has to offer you.

Over time, avoidance and safety behaviors deplete your self-confidence and make the world seem like a dangerous place. Eventually, you end up doing the things you once loved or working toward your goals due to the fear of being confronted with certain situations. However, your life is worth living and your fears shouldn't stop you from going after everything you dream of. Identifying your avoidance and safety behaviors is the first step to slowly letting go of them and developing the courage to endure difficulties.

Avoiding Avoidance

Have you ever caught yourself procrastinating or reacting to a situation in a passive-aggressive manner? Unconsciously, this was your way of avoiding dealing with a stressful situation or conversation. It's common to turn to avoidance behaviors because let's face it—dealing with stress is not fun! However, avoiding stress doesn't teach you how to manage stress effectively.

Consider procrastination. When you put off or delay doing something important due to the stress or anxiety the task may come with, you worsen your feelings of stress because in the back of your mind you know the task hasn't been completed. You will continue to feel anxious about the task until you eventually get it done. This example shows how ineffective avoidance behaviors are in helping you cope with stress. If anything, they can aggravate an already stressful situation, rather than give you the relief you need.

Here are a few reasons avoidance behaviors increase feelings of stress:

- Avoiding tasks or situations you can't back out of creates anxiety.

- When you avoid a certain situation you don't solve the problem, which means you continue to feel stressed even though you have distanced yourself from the situation.

- Avoiding conflict can compromise the quality of your relationships and create more conflict in the future.

- Avoidance causes problems to grow instead of proactively doing something to turn the situation around.

If you turn to avoidance behaviors during stressful situations, you can catch yourself in the act and replace your avoidant behaviors with healthy coping strategies. Bear in mind that it takes a lot of time and patience to completely eradicate your avoidance behaviors, especially when they have become habits. Therefore, be gentle with yourself as you follow these useful tips:

- **Understand what avoidance coping looks like.** The first step is to learn how to recognize when you are responding to a situation with avoidant behavior. Think of common scenarios where you tend to procrastinate, shut down, or block out what is happening. Make note of these scenarios and try to catch yourself when you are doing it.

- **Identify active coping strategies.** When you catch yourself doing avoidant behaviors, you can pause, reflect on your behavior, and replace it with an active coping strategy. An active coping strategy is any behavior that can help you reframe your thoughts, identify resources you didn't realize you had, and approach the situation from a positive standpoint.

- **Find healthier ways to relieve stress.** It's important to note that when you turn to avoidant behaviors, you are reacting due to feeling stressed. Instead of avoiding your stressful feelings, you can create a list of go-to stress-relief techniques that will calm your mind and body. Your stress-relief techniques could involve physical activity, like running or playing sports, or they could promote relaxation, like practicing breathing techniques or journaling.

- **Improve your communication skills.** Rather than running away from conflict, you can learn to resolve conflict by discussing your problems. If speaking to the person who has hurt you feels too confrontational, you can speak to a psychologist who can listen to you as you express your feelings. Discussing your problems is empowering because it gives you an opportunity to work through your strong emotions, express your boundaries, and create a win-win scenario in your relationships.

- **Learn to ask for help.** Seeking professional help is a sign of strength. A mental health specialist can teach you the skills and tools to identify and address unhealthy behaviors and negative thinking and learn how to cope with stress more effectively.

Exercise: Working Out Your Behaviors

When you are feeling anxious, it's a natural reaction to play it safe. Instead of seeking to understand or adjust to the situation, you revert to tried and tested behaviors that make you feel safe. Safety behaviors reinforce your fears and cause you to stay in your comfort zone. They also reinforce the belief that if it hadn't been for the use of your safety behaviors, you would be in trouble.

The truth is that safety behaviors create limitations in your life. They prevent you from learning how to overcome difficulties or challenging your fear-based thoughts. The false sense of safety these behaviors create is actually a trap that prevents you from living your life to the fullest.

Below is an example of a safety behavior at work and its consequence:

- You feel anxious among a group of friends

- To draw less attention to yourself, you avoid making eye contact or only speak when spoken to.

- This safety behavior offers you temporary relief from anxiety but makes it difficult for you to make friends.

Here is another example of safety behavior and its consequence:

- You feel self-conscious about your appearance.

- To make yourself feel better, you constantly check your appearance in the mirror.

- This safety behavior increases the pressure you feel to look a certain way and promotes harmful coping behaviors, like restricting food or constantly seeking validation about your appearance from others.

Now it's your turn. Create a list of the situations that normally cause you to feel anxious. This list could include personal, social, or environmental factors that make you anxious. Look at each item on your list and consider the safety behavior you turn to when feeling anxious. Write down the safety behavior next to the list item. For example:

- Feeling insecure about my looks = Wearing a lot of makeup to hide my imperfections

- I don't trust people = Avoid sharing personal information about me

- Nervous to speak in groups = Avoid groups of people so that I don't need to make conversation

Here are a few more safety behaviors that could be reactions to feeling anxious:

- Avoid making eye contact

- Over-preparing for presentations

- Mentally rehearsing conversations before they happen

- Always socializing with a friend by your side who does most of the talking

- Using drugs or alcohol when socializing with others to calm your anxious feelings

- Lying or exaggerating to make yourself look better

- Constantly checking on your phone in public to avoid social interactions

- Asking the person you are speaking to many questions to keep the focus off yourself

- Wearing a lot of clothing to cover your body or hiding your face with your hair

- Trying to appear as perfect as possible

- Trying very hard to please the people you are with to avoid rejection

Learning more about your safety behaviors can help you recognize when you are responding from a place of fear. This gives you an opportunity to choose a different response, perhaps one that can encourage you to step out of your shell a little bit more. For example, if you are nervous to speak in groups, you can practice making conversation with one or two individuals within a group to make conversing less intimidating.

Key Takeaways

Avoidance and safety behaviors have one purpose: To control your anxiety. However, instead of confronting and seeking to overcome the stressful situation, these behaviors create distance between you and the stressful situation. Thus, you end up blocking or putting off your feelings of anxiety, rather than finding a healthy way of coping with them. The first step in replacing avoidant and safety behaviors is recognizing when you are doing them. When you catch yourself in the act, you can pause, reflect on your behavior, and choose a better approach to dealing with your anxious feelings. In other words, instead of running away from the stressful situation, you can confront it by expressing how you are feeling, setting boundaries, journaling about your emotions, or reframing your negative thoughts.

Chapter 4:

Let's Create an Exposure

Ladder

In this chapter, you will learn:

- What is exposure therapy?
- How to create an exposure ladder.
- Helpful hints and tips for facing your fears.

What Is Exposure Therapy?

Exposure therapy is a type of behavioral therapy that seeks to help you face your fears. As we have already discussed in the previous chapter, when you are faced with a stressful situation, your natural reaction may be to avoid it. Exposure therapy can help you break the cycle of avoidance by gradually exposing you to the very thing you are running away from, in a safe environment. Through gradual exposure, you can start to become comfortable with those situations that you were previously uncomfortable with.

Exposure therapy is often used by psychologists as a tool to help you overcome various phobias, social anxiety disorder, and generalized anxiety disorder. A special form of exposure therapy known as exposure and response prevention therapy is often used to reduce compulsions caused by obsessive-compulsive disorder (OCD).

There are many different kinds of techniques psychologists can use to administer exposure therapy. However, in general, the main purpose of these techniques is to expose you to your fears according to a fear hierarchy of "ladder." Each time you successfully face your fear on one level, the doctor will move you up a level and expose you to your fear with greater intensity, until eventually you can fully look at and confront your fear up close.

Here are a few techniques your doctor may employ:

1. Graded Exposure

This method involves exposing you to your fears, one step at a time. This method works well when you are trying to work through a phobia, like being afraid of elevators. The first step may be to look at a photo of an elevator and imagine you were in it. The second step may be to visit a shopping mall and walk past several elevators. Next, your doctor may ask you to go one floor up on an elevator, and so on, until you are able to go inside an elevator without being fearful.

2. Systematic Desensitization

With this method, your doctor may use relaxation techniques, like breathing exercises or meditation, to help you get comfortable with each step on the fear hierarchy. For example, while looking at the photo of an elevator, your doctor may take you through a relaxation technique to calm your mind and body, reducing stress and breaking any negative associations you may have with looking at an elevator. This means that instead of feeling anxious the next time you see an elevator, you will be calm and feel neutral about it.

3. Flooding

Flooding involves exposing you to the highest step or level of the fear hierarchy all at once. A psychologist may use this method when seeking to reduce the anxiety that interferes with your daily life, like commuting to school, studying, or interacting with other people. However, since this approach is aggressive, it is only used near the end of the anxiety treatment program when you have already reduced a significant amount of anxiety using other exposure therapy techniques.

Exposure therapy is useful when seeking to get over your fears quickly. The more you expose yourself to something uncomfortable, the less uncomfortable it becomes. It can also help you reduce the strong emotional response you have when confronting specific situations. For example, if you feel anxious whenever you need to study for a test, exposure therapy can help you reduce the intense worry or fear you have while studying and make the process more engaging and productive.

Exposure therapy can also prove to you that some of your fears are irrational and aren't as exaggerated as you make them out to be. This is an important step in overcoming your fears because it helps you create a new story in your mind about what you are experiencing and how much of a risk it is. For example, if you are afraid of making new friends, putting yourself out there, in a safe environment, and striking conversations with different kinds of people can prove to you that you are capable of making friends and that doing so isn't as scary as you thought it would be.

Exercise: Create an Exposure Ladder

The most comfortable way to face your fears is to gradually expose yourself to the thing you fear the most. Creating a fear ladder can help you identify a fear that you wish to overcome and create a step-by-step plan to gradually expose yourself to the fear until you can confront it without being afraid. All it takes to create a fear ladder is three steps:

Step 1: Think of a Stressful or Difficult Task That You Avoid

Take a moment and think about a stressful or difficult task that you tend to avoid. This could be studying for major tests, presenting a speech in front of the classroom, or putting yourself out there in social situations. Pick a task that is important but you often avoid due to the stress or fear it brings.

Step 2: Set a Goal

Now that you have a task you desire to confront, the next step is to create a meaningful goal that clearly describes what you want to do (be specific), when or where you want to do it, and how much you want to do it. Here are a few examples to help you set your personal goals:

- Dedicate time to study for your test, at home after school, for 45 minutes 3 times a week.

- Strike a conversation with one classmate, during recess, for at least 5 minutes.

- Do a physical workout, at home after school, for 20 minutes 3 times a week.

Step 3: Create Steps to Achieve Your Goal

This step requires you to tap into your creative mind and think of really encouraging steps you can take to make working toward your goal fun and something you look forward to. These steps should make working toward your goal easier and feel less stressful or difficult. You can also rank the difficulty of each step on a scale of 0–10 (zero being extremely easy and 10 being extremely difficult) so you can organize your steps from easiest to most difficult. When sorting your steps, ensure that your final step is as close as possible to your goal. Here are a few examples to show you how to do it:

Goal: Overcome my fear of swimming at school

1. Watch other people swimming in the pool (rating 1/10)

2. View YouTube tutorials about swimming (rating 1/10)

3. Sit on the edge of the pool and put my feet in (rating 3/10)

4. Stand waist-deep in the shallow end (rating 5/10)

5. Hold your breath for 10 seconds underwater (rating 6/10)

6. Jump into the shallow from outside of the pool (rating 8/10)

7. Sign up for swimming lessons (rating 9/10)

Goal: Overcome dependency on social media, at home and school, during the week

1. Read about the consequences of technology dependency (rating 2/10)

2. Put your notifications on silent (rating 4/10)

3. Turn off your cell phone for an hour (rating 5/10)

4. Turn off your cell phone after a certain time in the evening (rating 7/10)

5. Call your friends to check on them rather than sending texts (rating 8/10)

6. Create one social media posting day a week and one day to respond to notifications (rating 9/10)

Goal: Overcome my obsession with my appearance, in public, every time I go out

1. Go out in public without wearing any accessories (rating 4/10)

2. Take 10 minutes to prepare before going out (time yourself to make sure you only spend 10 minutes getting ready) (rating 6/10)

3. Go out in public without brushing your hair (rating 7/10)

4. Go out in public without wearing any makeup, gel, perfume/cologne, etc (rating 8.5/10)

5. Don't look at yourself in the mirror before going out or while you are out (rating 9/10)

6. Enjoy a messy meal while eating at a restaurant (rating 10/10)

Helpful Hints and Tips for Practicing Exposure Therapy

Facing your fears shouldn't be a once-off event. Ideally, you should be exposing yourself to the things you fear on a regular basis, at a pace and level that is most comfortable to you. Instead of focusing on how quickly you can overcome a fear, you should aim to progressively feel less strongly about your fear. Exposure therapy can be a really effective way to help you embrace your fears, but it takes a lot of patience and planning to get it right. Here are a few tips on how you can maximize exposure therapy to get the results you are looking for:

1. Getting into the Habit of Making Lists

Lists are a great way of taking what is in your mind and putting it on paper. When you write down lists about the people, situations, or places you are fearful of, you can get a better understanding of the limitations holding you back from living a fulfilling life. Making lists can also help you group fears together and create a comprehensive strategy to tackle a range of fears. For example, you might group the fear of speaking in public, fear of crowds, and the fear of being judged by others and categorize them as your social fears. Now you can think of actionable steps (creating your ladder) that can help you combat your social fears, and rate the difficulty of each step.

2. Create Opportunities to Face Your Fears

Your fear ladders are created to make facing your fears less overwhelming. However, if you don't complete the action steps, you won't get really far in overcoming your fears. Commit to completing each step of the ladder, even when the difficulty of a step makes you feel uncomfortable. Remember, the more exposure you get, the less uncomfortable each step becomes. Repeatedly engage in each step and increase the period of time you spend doing it. For example, you might start off having 2 minute conversations with new acquaintances, but gradually increase the duration of your conversations to 3 minutes, then 5 minutes, until you don't need to time yourself.

3. Rate Your Fear Level During the Exposure Journey

As you practice exposing yourself to your fears, refer back to your fear ladder and re-rate each step. Ideally, the more you expose yourself to your fears, the less difficult it should be to perform each step. If your level of difficulty hasn't changed despite exposing yourself to each step, assess whether you are reinforcing each step enough times. You might benefit from practicing each step more or for a longer period of time. Moreover, don't be discouraged if you have only been able to reach one or two steps on your ladder. Celebrate your milestone and continue working toward exposing yourself to the next step on your ladder.

4. Reward Courageous Behavior

There will be times when you surprise yourself by stepping outside your comfort zone and going above and beyond what is expected of you. For example, if your plan was to journal about your body image issues and you decided to go above and beyond your task by writing and publishing an article helping other young people who are dealing with body image issues, this would be something to stop and celebrate! Simply exposing yourself to your fears is enough, but doing more than is required of you is unbelievably brave! Make your rewards fun, personal, and positive so that you motivate yourself to display courageous behavior again in the future.

Facing Your Fears Form

Below is a simple form that you can replicate in your journal. You can complete this form every time you expose yourself to fear. Filling out this form will help to keep a record of your progress in overcoming your fear, and you can be encouraged when you start seeing your fears decreasing in intensity. Overall, this form will help you manage your anxiety in a healthy way and boost your self-confidence.

In your journal, fill out the following information:

1. Specific fear you seek to address

2. Initial and final fear ratings from 0—10 (zero being no fear and 10 being extreme fear)

3. Length of time of exposure

4. Lessons learned during exposure

5. Any changes in outlook or perception of your fear (optional)

Key Takeaways

You are capable of facing your fears and living beyond the limitations you have set for yourself. All it takes is the willingness to overcome a fear that interferes with your daily life and the persistence to repeatedly expose yourself to the thing you fear. When practicing exposure therapy, slow and steady wins the race. You don't need to expose yourself to your fear all at once. Just take small steps that progressively move you closer and closer to finally coming face-to-face with your fear. Hopefully, after many sessions of exposure, you will come to realize that what you were once fearful of is actually not that threatening after all.

Chapter 5:

Other Ways to Combat Anxiety

In this chapter, you will learn:

- Alternative methods to help you combat symptoms of anxiety.

- How to use trial and error to find a method that works best for you!

Five Main Ways to Help Your Anxiety

It's common to feel anxious from time to time, but your anxious feelings don't have to run your life. When you are faced with difficult challenges that push you outside of your comfort zone or raise many hidden fears, you can learn how to stand tall and confront these challenges with confidence. Here are five effective ways of managing your anxious feelings:

Become a Pro at Relaxation

When you are placed under a stressful situation, your body naturally goes into fight-or-flight mode. This is when the stress response kicks in and your sympathetic nervous system activates. When your nervous system is triggered, your heart rate accelerates, muscles constrict, and blood pressure increases. The fight-or-flight mode is only useful when it is short-lived. If it lasts too long, it can compromise your mental and physical health.

Even though you can't avoid being in stressful situations, you can learn how to regulate your nervous system during times of stress. One of the best ways to do this is by teaching yourself to relax when you feel your heart rate rapidly increasing and your body tightening up. Breathing is as essential to your survival as water, and it can also help you relax your nervous system.

Deeper, slower, and longer breaths have the ability to reduce stress, slow down the pace of your thoughts, and put you at ease. Think about the moments when you feel relaxed. Are you breathing heavily or is your breathing slow and barely noticeable? When you take deep breaths, you force your mind and body to calm down and this can relieve tension and stress. You can practice how to take slower and deeper breaths by doing a few breathing exercises whenever you find yourself in a challenging situation.

Here are three breathing exercises you can practice at home:

1. Belly Breathing

Belly breathing is the simplest breathing exercise you can practice to instantly feel calm. To practice belly breathing follow these steps:

- Sit down in a comfortable position on the floor or on a chair.

- Place one hand on your chest and another hand on your belly (under your rib cage).

- Take a deep, slow breath through your nose and direct the breath to your belly. You should feel the hand on your belly move out, but the hand on your chest should remain in the same position.

- Breath out through your mouth, forming your lips like you are whistling. Let your breath out slowly and notice the hand on your belly move back in.

- Repeat this breathing process, paying attention to your hand on your belly moving out and in. The deeper and slower your breaths are, the more relaxed you will feel.

2. 4–7–8 Breathing

This next breathing exercise also uses belly breathing to help you relax, however, you are required to hold and release your breath for a certain amount of counts. Here are the steps to practice the 4–7–8 breathing exercise:

- Get yourself in a comfortable position, either on the floor or on a chair.

- Similar to the belly breathing exercise, put one hand on your chest and another hand on your belly.

- Take a deep and slow breath through your nose and direct your breath to your belly. As you inhale, count up to four in your mind. Notice your hand on your belly moving out, but ensure the hand on your chest stays in the same position.

- Hold your breath for another seven counts (count up to seven while holding your breath).

- Slowly release your breath through your mouth, forming your lips like you are whistling. As you breathe out, count up to eight in your mind, and feel your hand on your belly move back in.

- Continue breathing in and out until you feel relaxed.

3. Morning Breathing

The purpose of the morning breathing exercise is to help you get as much air into your lungs and relieve any muscle tension in your body so you can maximize your feeling of relaxation. Here are the steps to follow:

- Stand up tall with your knees slightly bent. Bend your upper torso forward toward your feet. Ensure that your arms are hanging loosely beside you and your shoulders are relaxed.

- Take a deep breath through your nose and slowly bring your upper torso to the normal standing position. As you come up, roll your back slowly so you can stretch every muscle, ending with your neck.

- Hold your breath for a few moments in the standing position.

- As you return back down toward your feet, exhale through your mouth.

- Repeat this breathing exercise until you feel relaxed.

Other than practicing breathing exercises, you can induce a feeling of relaxation by practicing meditation. Meditation is an ancient Eastern practice that has been adopted in the West and used as a tool to calm the mind and reduce stress. When you meditate, you take a moment to focus on your breathing, on an object in the room, or on any recurring thoughts in your mind. Having a single focus (or focusing on nothing at all) has a relaxing effect on the mind.

Since the mind naturally wanders to the past and to the future, it can be difficult to make it focus on whatever is occurring in the present moment. It is the same as trying to make a child who has eaten a lot of candy sit still. However, the more times you practice meditation, the easier it becomes to still the mind and lower stress and anxiety.

As you go through life, you will be faced with situations that require you to take a moment and think before you respond. Acting impulsively during these moments may cause you to make the wrong choices, say the wrong words, or behave inappropriately. Having the ability to quieten your mind and simply pause to think becomes your superpower! For instance, instead of avoiding uncomfortable emotions, you can pause and experience the impact of your emotions on your mind and body.

This superpower can be learned with meditation. However, progress doesn't happen overnight. Teach yourself to enjoy the process of being more present and focused on what is happening right here at this moment, or pausing to think about your experiences. With time, you will become a better meditator and will have the power to control your mind, rather than allow your mind to control you.

Here are simple steps that can help you learn how to meditate:

- Find a quiet room to sit in for a few minutes, with limited distractions.

- Sit down on the floor or on a chair and make sure you are comfortable.

- Take out your cell phone and set a time limit. Since you are a beginner, you can set the alarm to ring after 5—10 minutes.

- Gently close your eyes and focus on your breathing. If you want to, you can do a short breathing exercise to ease you into your meditation.

- Your breathing will be the focus of this meditation. Whenever your mind wanders to another place (past or future) or to any thought (positive or negative), simply return your focus to your breathing.

- Don't judge yourself or feel bad if you get distracted many times. Remember, your mind is still learning how to be comfortable being present. All you need to do is bring your attention back to your breathing.

- When your alarm goes off, take a few deep breaths and gently open your eyes. Before you stand up, notice how your body is feeling, your current mood, and any thoughts you have about your meditation.

Breathing exercises and practicing meditation can be effective ways to relax your mind and body. However, these two options don't require any movement. If you are somebody who enjoys being active, you may be interested in the practice of yoga. Yoga is a physical exercise that brings about a feeling of relaxation through each yoga pose. There are a number of different yoga poses, each ranging in level of difficulty. These poses can help you relieve tension in your body, improve blood circulation, regulate your breathing, and lower feelings of stress and anxiety.

All you will need to get started with yoga is form-fitting clothing and a yoga mat. Below are a few beginner-friendly yoga poses you can try:

1. **Mountain Pose**

Stand with your feet together and arms hanging at your side. Ensure that your feet are firmly rooted to the ground and that you are stable. Take a deep breath in, tighten your thigh muscles and stretch out your arms, raising them up until they are slightly behind your head. Ensure that your chest is open and your stomach tucked in. As you breathe out, loosen your shoulders and slowly begin to drop your arms until they are back to your sides. You can now loosen your thigh muscles and empty all of the breath in your belly.

2. Child's Pose

Sit down in a kneeling position with your feet tucked under your buttocks. Take a deep breath in and raise your arms toward the sky. As you breathe out, lower your arms in front of you and bend your upper body forward. Your belly should be resting on your thighs, your head tucked in, and arms extended in front of you.

3. Cat Pose

Go on all fours (hands and knees on the floor) and make sure your back is straight. Take a deep breath in and as you breathe out, round your spine and tuck your head toward your chest. When you breathe in again, slowly go from a rounded spine to an arched back and lift your head toward the ceiling. As you exhale, round your spine again.

4. Downward-Facing Dog

Go on all fours again, although this time your hands and feet should be touching the ground, not your knees. Extend your legs back until you are forming a V-shape with your buttocks at the highest point. Your feet should be hip-distance apart and your chest should be tucked and pointed toward your legs.

5. Corpse Pose

To wrap up your yoga session, you can practice the corpse pose. This is the simplest to do because it requires you to lie down on your back with your feet slightly apart and your arms resting by your sides, palms facing upward. The back of your thighs, buttocks, and back should be rested firmly on the ground. While you are in this position, close your eyes and try to relax your mind.

Get Plenty of Sleep, Nourishment and Exercise

Did you know that getting poor quality sleep can increase your risk of getting an anxiety disorder? Alternatively, if you are already living with an anxiety disorder, you could be at a higher risk of experiencing sleep disorders like insomnia. You need sufficient, uninterrupted sleep to increase your mental and emotional well-being. Sleep disturbances or sleep deprivation can make you feel restless, irritable, and stressed.

The best way to ensure that you are getting good sleep is to adopt healthy sleeping habits. Here are three that you can start practicing today:

1. Create a Sleeping Schedule

When setting a sleeping schedule, the first step is to decide on how many hours you need to sleep so you can wake up feeling rested. In general, teenagers between the ages of 13 and 18 need between 8 to 10 hours of sleep in a 24 hour period. Depending on how many hours you need, determine the best time to go to bed.

If it usually takes you a while before falling asleep, go to bed at least an hour before your bedtime and ensure your mobile device is switched off or in another room. Now all you will need to do is go to bed at the same time each night to train your body to follow the new sleeping schedule. Don't panic if it takes you a while to get into your new schedule. Your consistency is what will help your body learn the new sleep and wake cycle. On weekends, avoid going to bed later than an hour after your bedtime, otherwise, this might interrupt your schedule.

2. Pay Attention to Your Diet

As a general rule of thumb, you should avoid going to bed on an empty or full stomach. In both instances, you will find it difficult to fall asleep. After 3 p.m. in the afternoon, avoid drinking beverages high in sugar content or caffeine, as it may take a while before the buzz wears off.

3. Create a Bedtime Routine

To complement your sleeping schedule, you can create a bedtime routine. This is simply a number of relaxing activities you have picked out that can help you calm your mind and body before bed. There are many different kinds of activities you might find relaxing, like reading a book, taking a hot shower, journaling, or meditating. Pick a few of your favorites and give yourself enough time to practice each one so you aren't in a rush. Make sure that your environment encourages sleep by dimming your lights, avoiding technology, or playing soothing music softly in the background.

Another lifestyle change that can help you manage your anxiety is eating a balanced diet. According to doctors, there are foods that are known to reduce symptoms of anxiety due to the nutrients they contain. These foods include:

- Brazil nuts are high in selenium, which is an essential mineral that can improve your mood, reduce inflammation, and treat anxiety and depression symptoms. Besides brazil nuts, you can find selenium in other nuts and foods like mushrooms and soybeans.

- Fatty fish, such as salmon, mackerel, trout, and herring have a high concentration of omega-3 fatty acids, which have been found to improve cognitive function and maintain good mental health. Consuming at least two servings of fatty fish a week can improve symptoms of anxiety.

- Egg yolks are a great source of vitamin D. A deficiency in vitamin D has been linked to mood disorders like anxiety and depression. Eggs also contain an amino acid called tryptophan, which is used by the brain to produce serotonin. Serotonin is a chemical neurotransmitter that improves brain function, regulates your moods, and can help you relieve symptoms of anxiety.

- Pumpkin seeds contain a high amount of potassium that helps you balance your body's supply of electrolytes and stabilize blood pressure. Foods that are rich in potassium, such as pumpkin seeds or bananas can reduce symptoms of stress and anxiety.

- Turmeric is a spice often used in Thai and Indian cuisine. It contains an ingredient called curcumin that reduces inflammation and oxidative stress, two conditions that are normally prevalent in people who are anxious or depressed. While turmeric is typically added in savory dishes, you can pour some of the spice into your smoothies too.

- Chamomile tea is a natural herbal remedy that has anti-inflammatory and anti-anxiety properties. The soothing effect of chamomile tea comes from the flavonoids found in the tea, which can help you feel calm, and even induce sleep.

Once your sleeping schedule is underway and you're eating a healthy anti-anxiety diet, you can further boost your brain health by incorporating physical exercise into your lifestyle. Take a moment and think about how many times you break a sweat in a week. Is it every day? Twice a week? Or never? There is a direct link between living an active lifestyle and improved mental health. For example, research suggests that physical exercise can be as effective as antidepressants when treating mild to moderate depression (Better Health Channel, 2012). Physical exercise can also be used alongside other treatments like CBT when managing stress and anxiety.

Ideally, you should be getting at least 30 minutes of moderate exercise a day. This may sound like a lot of time, but if you switch up your physical activity each day, you can make working out fun! Here are a few fun physical activities to try out:

- Play a walking/running game like "Zombies, Run!" where you are placed in the middle of a Zombie apocalypse and Zombies chase you as you attempt to gather as many supplies for your neighborhood.

- Have a dance party in your bedroom and put on a playlist of your favorite songs. Make sure you move your body and while you're at it—practice a few TikTok dance moves!

- Design your own workout routine by incorporating all of your favorite upper and lower body exercise positions.

- Grab a friend (or pet) and play frisbee outside. Challenge yourself to throw a frisbee, going back and forth, without dropping it on the ground.

- Instead of going on the elevator, take the stairs and work out your glutes and legs.

- Organize a hike with your family or friends and use it as an opportunity to bond while getting a healthy workout in.

- Volunteer to take your dog for a walk around your neighborhood.

- Think of a sport you have always wanted to do. Get the right gear and attend a practice. You can also inquire about running or cycling clubs that you can join within your community.

- Jumping on a trampoline can be considered moderate physical exercise. If you don't have a trampoline at home, you can visit a trampoline center!

Connect With Others

Spending time with your friends and family not only guarantees laughter but can also positively impact your mental health. Humans are naturally social creatures that rely on the support received from others to relieve stress, make positive choices about our lives, and increase self-esteem. When you find yourself having doubts or thinking about troubling thoughts, speaking to someone you trust can make you walk away with a greater sense of control and self-confidence.

If you desire to be supported by others, you need to be open to the idea of connecting with people—first those closest to you, and eventually branching out and getting to know different people. It's important to remind those dear to you that you care about them and are willing to get to know them better. You can convey this message by spending quality time with your loved ones and showing them that you prioritize your relationship.

Whether you desire to connect with your friends or family, there are a few fun ways you can go about it:

- Host a games night

- Host a pool party

- Cook a meal from a recipe book

- Host a book club meeting

- Try a new adventurous activity

- Workout together

- Pick a few topics from a jar and talk about them

- Read a book in silence together

- Host a movie night

- Catch up on a TV series

You might be interested in getting to know your friends and family better, but aren't quite sure what to talk about. The best way to get anyone to open up more is to ask them questions, however, every now and again, you can also offer your own opinion and keep the conversation bouncing back and forth.

Here are a few questions that will help you start a conversation with someone you wish to get to know better:

Conversation Starters About School

- Which subject are you currently enjoying at school? What do you like about it?

- Are you part of a sports team in school?

- If you become a teacher for a day, how would you run your classroom?

- If there was one thing you would change about your school, what would it be?

Conversation Starters About Hobbies and Interests

- Do you have any hobbies?

- Do you play video games? Which ones are you into right now?

- Do you know how to play a musical instrument?

- How do you like to spend your weekends?

- What type of music do you enjoy listening to?

- What is your favorite movie of all time?

- Do you have any special talents or skills?

Conversation Starters About Friends and Family

- What do you think makes someone a good friend?

- Do you like hanging around with a few friends or in a large group of friends?

- How strict are your parents?

- Do you have any siblings? How many?

- What do you love most about your family?

Conversation Starters About Romantic Relationships

- Do you have a crush on anybody right now?

- What do you look for in a boyfriend/girlfriend?

- Are your friends in romantic relationships?

- If you could marry a celebrity, which celebrity would it be?

Conversation Starters About Future Goals

- Is there anything that scares you about the future?

- Do you know what you want to do after you graduate?

- What is your dream job?

- If you could live anywhere in the world, where would you live?

- Do you have any role models?

Connect With Nature

While connecting with other people is rewarding, connecting to nature can also help you feel whole and balanced. Seeing the lush greenery, tumbling with your dog outside, and enjoying the cool breeze—are all calming outdoor activities that can improve your mood, lower your stress and anxiety, and help you feel more connected to nature. The reason why connecting to nature is so relaxing and grounding is because of its simplicity. You don't have to think, work, or talk when you are outdoors, just appreciate the sounds, sights, smells, and sensations around you.

The first step when connecting to nature is to get outside. You could be in your own backyard, in a nearby park, or on a busy street. The second step is to take a few deep breaths and begin walking. As you walk, pay attention to each step you take, how your body moves, and how you feel being outdoors. Are there any interesting sights to see or people to watch? Can you distinguish between the different sounds that you hear? Now, check back with yourself. How are you feeling? Are you still feeling calm? As you continue to walk, engage your five senses (sight, hearing, smell, touch, and taste), and take in everything around you.

Instead of walking, you can also find a bench outside that you can sit on and observe everything taking place around you. This strategy normally works best in a busy area, like a shopping mall, beachfront, or local park. As you are sitting on the bench, you can watch the passers-by, connect to the different sounds, or simply enjoy the rays of sunlight or cool breeze hitting against your face.

When you get back home, you can journal about your experience in nature and what sensations, thoughts, memories, or emotions came up during your time outdoors. When your mind and body are relaxed, it's common for your mind to drift to the past and think about certain memories that your experience in nature reminds you of. Take a note of these memories and journal about them when you get back home.

Pay Attention to the Good Things

Gratitude is the act of showing appreciation for who you are, what you have, and the life you live. You can show gratitude for the small or large moments that make your day feel meaningful. Practicing gratitude has been shown to reduce stress and anxiety, and increase your emotional resilience.

When you are anxious, you may panic or start overthinking. This reaction increases your fear and triggers your body's stress response. Practicing gratitude in those moments can help you empathize with what you are going through and find ways of soothing your mind and body. For example, instead of saying to yourself, "You are acting weird!" you can say, "I notice you are uncomfortable and it's causing you to retreat in your shell." This shows a greater sense of appreciation for who you are and seeks to uplift you rather than pull you down.

Practicing gratitude can also help you root out negative self-talk and adopt healthier beliefs about yourself. When you find yourself entering a loop of negative thinking, you can pause and reframe your thoughts, choosing a more encouraging opinion or belief. For example, it's common to compare yourself to other people and conclude that they are superior to you. This kind of thought is negative because it seeks to pull you down. You can reframe this thought by saying to yourself, "I have my personal strengths which make me powerful." Then, go ahead and think about a few strengths that are unique to you and make a positive impact in your life (such as your ability to make people laugh, how smart you are, or how good you are at basketball).

There are three ways you can begin practicing gratitude on a daily basis:

1. Pay Attention to the Goodness in Your Life

Life is full of positive and negative circumstances, but in general, people have the tendency to focus on negative circumstances. This is because we are so afraid of experiencing pain that we would rather anticipate negative situations happening than anticipate positive situations taking place. It takes a lot of time and patience to train your brain to notice the good things that occur in your life and how much of an impact they make. Each day, write down three things that you are grateful for in your journal. Try to list different things every day, and at the end of the week, notice how many good things (big and small) occur in your life.

2. Enjoy the Feeling of Gratitude

Have you ever held the door for an old person, donated clothes to an orphanage, or performed a random act of kindness? Do you remember how good it felt when you put a smile on someone's face? In essence, that is how gratitude feels. When you are grateful for who you are or what you have, you can feel a deep sense of excitement. Your brain enjoys this feeling so much that it will look for more ways to practice gratitude just so it can trigger the same feeling again. Whenever you catch yourself feeling excited about your life, take the time to absorb this feeling while it lasts.

3. Learn How to Express Gratitude

Expressing gratitude is more than saying "please" or "thank you." It's about communicating how much you appreciate something or someone. For example, you can show gratitude to your friends by telling them how much you appreciate their support. Or you can show gratitude to your teachers by thanking them for a really informative lesson. In other words, expressing gratitude is about noticing something good and paying a genuine compliment or doing something kind as a token of your appreciation.

Remember that when you show gratitude, you are doing so with no expectation of receiving anything in return. You do something kind or pay a compliment because it is your way of showing appreciation. It's about making someone else feel good because of how good they have made you feel about yourself.

Key Takeaways

Besides going to psychotherapy or taking medication, there are many different lifestyle interventions you can make to manage your anxiety. These include learning how to self-soothe through practicing relaxation, getting sufficient sleep and eating anti-anxiety foods, living an active lifestyle, and spending more time outdoors. Be sure to also take time to pause and savor the good things that occur in your life—you may need to look harder to find them but your effort is worth the reward of feeling good about yourself! Now that you know healthy alternatives to managing anxiety, let's look at some healthy alternatives for managing depression.

Chapter 6:

Kicking Depression to the Curb

In this chapter, you will learn:

- A variety of methods that you can use to overcome your depressive symptoms.

- Five coping mechanisms for managing depression and 20 practical ways to kick depression to the curb, starting right now!

Five Coping Mechanisms to Overcome Depressive Symptoms

When you are feeling depressed, it isn't easy to just "snap out of it." Since depression is a mental illness, it influences how you see yourself and your life. It can make you perceive normal tasks that you used to carry out with ease as being extremely exhausting or difficult or make you feel disinterested in being around people—even if you used to be the life of the party.

It is also difficult to tell when you will overcome your depressive symptoms since they can drain your energy and leave you feeling unmotivated to pick yourself up and make progress in your life. However, generally speaking, the actions that you feel the least motivated to do (such as socializing, creating a routine, or getting outside of your comfort zone), can be the very actions that slowly help you recover from depression.

In this chapter, you will learn four coping mechanisms that can help you overcome depressive symptoms. Practicing these coping mechanisms won't feel fun and certainly won't be easy because they challenge you to act against your feelings of hopelessness, fatigue, or anxiety. You may not have the energy to practice these coping mechanisms, but even the smallest of steps in the right direction can help.

As you practice these coping mechanisms, check-in with yourself and notice how you are feeling. Even though it is good to step outside of your comfort zone and do things that require courage, be careful not to push yourself too hard. If you need more time to prepare yourself mentally or physically to carry out these coping mechanisms, it is okay to do so. At the end of the day, you are in charge of your recovery and it is always best to go at your own pace.

Reach Out to Someone You Trust

One of the biggest factors in overcoming depressive symptoms is reaching out for help. This is because depression has a way of isolating you or making you feel like you are the only person in the world going through a difficult time. Speaking to someone you trust can offer you the emotional support you need, as well as the reassurance that you are not alone and that what you are experiencing is normal.

The first people to reach out to you would be your immediate families, such as your grandparents, parents, or older siblings. These people generally know you better than anyone else and can be a great source of support. If you don't have strong relationships with your immediate family members, you can reach out to extended family members like aunts and uncles, or community members like your favorite school teacher, coach, or counselor. If none of these people can provide you with the support you need, there are plenty of free hotlines you can call and speak to a professional mental health specialist. Otherwise, if you prefer texting, you can join free age-appropriate forums and support groups where you can receive support from other teens who are going through the same experiences as you.

In most cases, what makes it difficult to reach out to someone is the fear of sharing your feelings. You may be afraid of being judged or ridiculed for what you are going through. Remember that similar to anxiety, depression can create irrational fears that are not based on truth. In other words, your fear that others may judge your feelings is simply an assumption, not a fact. You may also find it easier to talk about your depression once you have accepted your own feelings, without judging yourself. Remind yourself that being depressed doesn't mean that you are weak, flawed, or strange in any way. The mental illness you are struggling with is experienced by millions of teenagers across the world, thus you are not alone.

If you are not sure how to go about reaching out to others, here is a list of five things you can do to get started:

- Find one person to open up to about your feelings.

- Dedicate a day out of your weekend to volunteer at a shelter.

- Walk your dog with a friend.

- Schedule a catch-up FaceTime session with your close friend or relative once a week.

- Find a community member you trust and open up about your struggle with depression.

Spend More Time on Things That Make You Feel Good

Depression tends to lower your moods, drain your energy, and cause you to lose interest in everyday activities. One way to fight against depression is to fill up your time with tasks that make you feel good. The goal is to go to bed each night having done at least one thing that day that made you smile. Try not to force yourself to have fun or do things just for the sake of pushing yourself. Take time to think about the small actions you can take—that are within your means—that will make you feel good about yourself. On some days, you might enjoy writing a piece of poetry, and on other days your highlight will be playing with your dog or calling an old friend.

Adopt Healthy Habits

Since depression can make you feel like you are not in control of your mind, taking the time to customize your lifestyle and incorporate healthy habits that promote good health can alleviate depressive symptoms. By now, you probably know what a healthy lifestyle consists of eating healthy foods, getting enough sleep, and making sure you exercise regularly. All of these practices are effective in reducing your stress levels and improving your moods. It's also important to avoid drugs and alcohol when you are treating depression. Even though drugs and alcohol give you a temporary boost of energy and confidence, they can cause you to sink deeper into depression once the "high" wears off. If you are looking for healthier habits to practice that can uplift your mood and boost your levels of confidence, why not try a few of these:

- Spend a day in nature

- Write down a list of your strengths

- Read a book

- Listen to your favorite musician

- Grab your favorite snacks and watch a blockbuster movie

- Burn scented candles and take a relaxing bath

- Switch off your phone and have a tech-free day

Find Proactive Ways to Manage Stress and Anxiety

When stress and anxiety are not addressed properly, they can lead to depression. Think about it: How drained or emotionally withdrawn would you feel if you were exposed to stress on an ongoing basis? Constant stress, doubt, and fear can increase anxiety levels and eventually trigger depression. Finding ways of managing your stress and anxiety can improve depressive symptoms and make it easier to cope with difficulties in your life. Here are a few examples of being proactive in how you manage stress and anxiety:

- If you are approaching a deadline, but you haven't made much progress on your task, reach out to your teacher and express the difficulty you are experiencing. Ask for advice on how you can manage your time better, or if you are having trouble understanding the task instructions, ask for more clarity.

- If you suspect that you have a health concern, like a substance abuse problem or pregnancy scare, find an adult you can trust and let them know what you are going through. If you are afraid of speaking to your parents, reach out to your school counselor or nurse.

- If you have noticed that you are struggling to make friends or connect with your family members, speak to a family therapist or counselor and ask them to help you learn effective communication skills.

Challenge Your Negative Thoughts

After depression tries to isolate you, it can make you turn against yourself. How? Without the positive assurance of others, you are left to make sense of your own experiences. In most cases, you perceive yourself or your life in a negative light and these thoughts can make you feel more separated from others. You might think to yourself, "The reason I don't have friends is that I'm a bad person" or "No one notices how much pain I am in because no one cares."

When you constantly think negatively about yourself or your life, you may struggle to ask for help or talk about your depression. Your negative self-perception causes you to feel ashamed of your negative thoughts and feelings, which makes it harder to speak about them. Since depression often puts a negative twist on things, you can combat your depressive symptoms by learning how to challenge your negative thoughts.

The first step in challenging your negative thoughts is noticing that what you think or feel isn't always true. Yes, the feeling or thought may be intense, but it isn't always a reflection of what is happening in reality. Once you are aware that your thoughts and feelings aren't always true, you can examine them closely and identify which thoughts are actually worsening your depressive symptoms. Below are a few types of thoughts that are negative and can aggravate your depression:

- **All-or-nothing thinking:** Having extreme opinions or expectations about situations, such as expecting to get an A+ on all your subjects at school or thinking that if someone isn't talking to you they are angry with you.

- **Overgeneralization:** Basing your opinion about what is happening now on a single negative experience that happened in the past. For instance, if you failed an entrance exam last summer, you think that you will likely fail again this time around.

- **Mental filtering:** Overlooking the positive aspects of a situation and focusing all your attention on the negative aspects. For instance, you may forget about all the acts of kindness your friend has shown over the past few months and judge them harshly on a single mistake.

- **Jumping to conclusions:** Assuming that a situation will turn out negatively or that someone doesn't like you without having any facts to back up your claim. For example, you might decide to reject an invitation to a party because you think it will be boring or you won't have anyone to talk to. These are assumptions you make about your experience at the party, not facts.

- **Emotional reasoning:** Having a strong belief that just because you have a bad feeling about something, that is the truth about the situation. For instance, you may feel uncomfortable with the idea of going out with your friends and believe that your feeling is a sign to stay at home.

- **Labeling:** Name-calling yourself due to negative experiences from the past. For instance, you might call yourself a 'loser' because you never had a large group of friends in high school, or if you failed a grade or never made it into a sports team, you might believe you are a 'failure.'

Once you have identified your negative thoughts, it's time to challenge them with cold hard facts. Any thought that cannot be proven with factual evidence to be true, must be an assumption you are making. Here are four questions you can ask yourself to challenge every negative thought that comes to your mind:

- What evidence do I have to prove this thought is true?

- What evidence do I have to prove this thought is false?

- What advice would I give to a friend who had this thought?

- Is there another way of looking at this situation that I might be missing?

- If I didn't have depression, how differently would I look at this situation?

The more you challenge your negative thoughts, the more obvious it will become that they were simply negative ideas you had in your mind, not real experiences related to your life.

Twenty Things to Try Today to Fight Against Depression

Fighting against depression takes small, but consistent, baby steps. You may not feel better after the first week of recovery, or the second week, but eventually, the small lifestyle choices you make will pay off.

Below are 20 things that you can try in your efforts to manage your depressive symptoms and regain a sense of control over your mind. These strategies can support a healthy lifestyle and are safe to practice at home. Remember to check in with yourself often as you work through recovery to ensure you are not pushing yourself too hard.

Have an open mind and enjoy the improved well-being you experience as a result of constantly practicing these 20 activities!

1. Meet Yourself Where You Are

Depression is more prevalent nowadays in society, particularly with young people, due to the increasing social pressures young people are faced with. It's become common to hear of a young person, regardless of their background, battling depression. When seeking to recover from depression, it's important to know that you are not alone. There are millions of young people, sharing similar experiences to you, who are also overcoming similar obstacles.

Remind yourself often that you are not strange, weak, or undesirable just because you are suffering from mental illness. On days when you feel discouraged, think about the many other teens who are going through the same experiences as you are. Let this thought encourage you to take things easy, speak kind words about yourself and your life, and have hope that your mental well-being will improve with time.

What does it mean to meet yourself where you are? It means accepting your life circumstances, rather than being ashamed of them or feeling guilty that you can't live a certain way. Instead of wishing you were someone else or had a completely different experience, meeting yourself where you are is about showing yourself compassion during your time of need. Even if you have a strong support system, at the end of the day you are your own best friend. No one else can comfort you, encourage you, and help you get through bad days as well as you can.

To learn how to accept your life circumstances and show compassion for your mental illness, you can write yourself letters in your journal. In previous chapters, we have mentioned how effective journaling can be in processing uncomfortable thoughts and emotions and giving you a peek into your inner life. Journaling can also help you build a stronger relationship with yourself by frequently writing yourself loving and encouraging messages of support.

Journaling is also the perfect excuse to tap into your creative mind. If writing long essays is not your thing, you can write yourself a poem, song, or fictional story representing your life, where you are the main character. While there are no rules when it comes to journaling, there is one thing you need to remember: Journaling is a judgment-free zone. If you are writing about negative thoughts, avoid judging them or labeling yourself as "nasty" or "embarrassing." All of your thoughts and emotions (good or bad) are valid and deserve the space to be felt and acknowledged. The more you learn to express whatever you have on your mind without holding back, the more you will learn to accept who you are and develop trust in yourself.

If you are interested in getting started with journaling but aren't sure what to write about, here are a few journal prompts that will get your creative juices flowing:

- What are the top five things that are stressing you right now? Rate them in the order of priority, from most stressful to least stressful.

- What are some of the frequent emotions you feel when you are stressed? How do these emotions play out?

- When was the first time you realized that you may be depressed? Can you retell the story?

- How do you think your childhood upbringing has affected your mental health?

- What personal strengths have helped you manage your depression so far? Can you give examples of specific events where they were displayed?

- What are some of the positive phrases you have repeated to yourself that have kept you going?

- Amidst this challenging time, what are five things you are grateful for?

2. Be Down, But Don't Stay Down

It's natural to feel drained, numb, or disinterested in everyday activities when you are depressed. You can't help experiencing low moods or feeling overwhelmed by most tasks. It is also healthier to allow yourself to release these emotions than trying to suppress them and acting like everything is okay.

When you are feeling down, give yourself the time and space to feel down. Become acquainted with your feelings and make them feel welcome in your body. For example, when you sense that you are becoming irritable, you can say to yourself:

"Hi there, irritability! I see you are back again. What has triggered you this time?"

Remember that all of your emotions are valid, even the ones that seek to isolate you or pull you down. All they need is a little bit of your attention and they will gradually disappear again.

With all that said, you must create some sort of boundaries around your emotions so that you can manage how long you stay down. Without having these boundaries in place, your emotions may choose to stay activated in your body for longer than you are comfortable. For example, it's perfectly normal to feel angry, but without putting boundaries around your anger, you may continue to feel angry for days on end. Therefore, to manage your anger, you might say:

"Anger, I accept you and welcome you in my body. However, I am only giving you an hour to say or do whatever you need to. Thereafter, I need you to subside so I can feel calm and balanced again."

When you are down, remember to show yourself even more compassion. This is usually when you need positive reassurance the most. You would be surprised just how comforting it can be to hear yourself saying "Everything will be alright." You can also use this low moment in your day to get real with yourself and practice the T.R.U.T.H technique. Here is how you can practice telling yourself the truth:

T: Tell yourself the truth about what has upset you, in one sentence.

R: Recognize the emotions you are feeling.

U: Uncover self-critical thoughts that may be pulling you down or making it hard to accept your current situation.

T: Try to empathize with your self-critical thoughts by reflecting on where they might come from (i.e. past experiences, self-doubt, low self-esteem, childhood lessons, etc.)

H: Have acceptance for your uncomfortable emotions. Realize that they are not your enemy and they have not come to ruin your life. Instead, they have come to help you better understand your emotional experience at the moment.

3. Set Attainable Goals

Setting S.M.A.R.T goals can help you create structure in your day and set small recovery milestones that you can look forward to. Your goals don't have to be big or set for the future. You can create short-term goals like getting to bed at a certain time, completing your chores, or leaving the house for at least an hour a day. S.M.A.R.T goals are an acronym that stands for specific, measurable, achievable, relevant, and time-based. Here is how you can ensure your daily goals are S.M.A.R.T:

Specific: Your goal should have a clear who, what, where, and why. Take some time to think about your goal, the intention behind it, and what exactly it entails.

Measurable: Tracking your goal is important because it allows you to see how much progress you have made. By adding specific metrics like "completing five tasks" or "waking up at 7:30 a.m." you will be able to tell if you have achieved your goal or not.

Achievable: Your goal should push you out of your comfort zone, but it must be something you have the skills, time, and energy to do. Avoid setting goals that require certain resources that you don't have, or that are too difficult to reach.

Relevant: Goals that mean something to you and can benefit your life in a certain way are generally more motivating than goals that sound good on paper, but don't mean much to you. Make sure that your goal can positively impact your life and make you feel better about yourself.

Time-based: Putting a time limit on your goal gives the drive to work toward it each day. It also provides you with an indication of how much time you have to accomplish it. Knowing the exact time frame you are working with can reduce any anxiety related to pursuing your goal.

4. See Each Day as Being Different From the Last

An effective way to regulate your moods and give you a positive start to your day is to treat each day as being different from the last. In other words, when you wake up in the morning, you tell yourself that you have experienced a mental reset, and now you can start the day with new intentions, goals, and attitudes. What happened yesterday is behind you and isn't an indication of what will happen today. Moreover, yesterday's moods and hardships have been experienced and now are in the past. You have new opportunities today to do things that make you feel good and entertain positive thoughts that uplift your mood.

5. Assess Things in Separate Parts

Do you remember the fifth coping mechanisms we spoke about? How to challenge your negative thoughts? Well, one of the habits of negative thinking is overgeneralizing a situation. When you do this, you tend to think that the outcome of your current situation will be the same as the single negative experience you went through in the past. To avoid overgeneralization, you need to take the time to pause and analyze a situation for what it's worth.

Look at it from different angles and imagine how somebody else would respond if they were in your situation. Avoid focusing on the negative aspects of the situation only. Look deeper, and you will find positive things that can improve your perception of the situation. In other words, what you go through in life is never "all good" or "all bad;" there are both good and bad sides to every circumstance—it's up to you to choose whether you will be influenced by the good or bad things you see.

6. Empathize With Your Inner Critical Voice

The sneaky aspect of depression is that it causes you to turn against yourself, the more you entertain discouraging thoughts and beliefs about who you are or what you are capable of. Every person who suffers from depression knows about the "depression voice," which is the critical voice in the mind that affirms negative beliefs about a person's life. While it's normal to think critically about yourself from time to time when these thoughts become an everyday occurrence they can interfere with your daily life and compromise your routines or goals.

The inner critical voice can seem more powerful than you are and this can cause you to feel afraid of confronting it. However, you should remind yourself that your inner critical voice represents a part of you that is hurt, angry, afraid, or lonely. Since this part of you is in so much pain, it projects hurtful ideas and thoughts. Instead of being afraid of confronting this part of you, you can choose to empathize with the amount of pain it must be in.

For example, when you think to yourself, "You are ugly," you can stop, take a few deep breaths, and identify that this thought must come from a part of you—the inner critic—that is deeply hurt. Instead of judging the inner critic, you can show empathy for what it must be going through. In response to the thought, you could say, "I can feel how much pain you are carrying about your self-image and I am sorry that you feel this way."

By empathizing with your inner critical voice, you can separate yourself from your negative thoughts and see them as being a result of the unresolved emotions you are carrying. It can also be a reminder to you that there are parts of you that are still hurting and perhaps seeking professional counseling can help you heal these parts of yourself.

The voice of depression isn't the monster you might think it is. It is simply a part of you that is in pain. Are you able to be honest with yourself and recognize that you are carrying a lot of hurt? If so, then your inner critical voice becomes more of a friend, or at least an acquaintance, than a foe. The reason your inner critical voice shows up so often is that it is trying to get your attention and inform you about the psychological issues you may be experiencing. Take time to listen to your inner critical voice and show empathy for whatever it reveals to you.

7. Reward Your Efforts

Progress is progress, no matter how small it is. Every step you take in the right direction is worth acknowledging, even if you are simply acknowledging it to yourself. The truth is it takes a lot of courage to be open to recovery and the effort you put into managing your depressive symptoms deserves to be celebrated.

Rewarding your efforts isn't about throwing a big party and inviting all of your friends and family. In reality, it is a lot more personal and meaningful than that. When you reward your efforts, you deliberately stop what you are doing or thinking and take the time to appreciate how far you have come. Many people might not understand the sacrifices and personal struggles you have overcome (or continue to fight) to get to where you are today, so this moment is purely meant for you to reflect on your small victories.

How you show yourself appreciation is up to you! You can decide what a meaningful reward looks like, how big it is, how much money you spend (if you spend any money at all), and whether or not you would like to share the moment with anyone else. Here are a few ideas on ways you can reward yourself for the positive steps you are taking to recover from depression:

- Pour essential oils in a warm bath and soak in water for as long as you would like. Each essential oil has its own benefits, such as helping to boost your mood, relieve headaches, reduce inflammation, and minimize the sensation of pain. Each time you run yourself a bath, try a different essential oil and write about your experience afterward.

- Is there a snack you have been dying to try for a while that may not be considered "healthy?" When you reward yourself for your effort you can bend the rules and treat yourself to sugary snacks, a cool tech gadget or video game, or a trip to the shopping mall—anything indulgent that you wouldn't normally treat yourself to.

- Limit your screen time so that you can spend time on physical activities that feel meaningful. For example, if you enjoy swimming, you might decide to switch your cell phone off while you take a dip in the pool. Limiting your screen time gives you the chance to enjoy whatever task you are doing without interruptions.

- Visit the library or local bookstore and pick up a good book. It can be a book in your favorite genre or one that is in a new genre.

- Listen to soothing music or create a playlist with your favorite songs. If you are feeling creative, you can also create themed playlists that consist of songs to complement what you are feeling. For instance, if you are in a celebratory mood, you can put on your playlist with celebratory music, or when you are in a reflective mood, you can put on a playlist with meaningful songs.

- Organize your space and remove clutter that may be lying around. A clean and de-cluttered space can uplift your mood and give you a sense of control of your physical environment. You might decide to clean your room, reorganize your closet, or store away items that you no longer use.

- Get around people or watch shows that make you laugh. No one can deny how good it feels to laugh and feel light about life. If you haven't had a good laugh in a while, you can watch a stand-up comedy show, or sitcom, or reach out to your funny friend or relative.

8. Create a Routine

To prevent your depression from interfering with your daily schedule, you can create a comfortable routine that allows you to move at your own pace. Below are simple tips on how to create your personalized daily routine:

- Create a list of priority tasks that must be included in your routine, such as going to school, doing household chores, and so on.

- Identify the best times of the day to concentrate. For instance, if you are a morning person, you may schedule all the tasks that require focus in the morning.

- Create time blocks to carry out each task. Stick to either 10, 15, or 30-minute time blocks for each task. If you need more time per task, you can add another 10, 15, or 30 minutes.

- Set a timer before you start a task and switch it off after you have completed the task so that you get an idea of how long it takes you (on average) to complete certain tasks.

- Schedule rest breaks throughout the day so that you don't feel overwhelmed completing all of your tasks.

- Create a visual calendar that you can mark with colors after you have completed a task. This will help you keep track of your progress and determine how well you are sticking to your routine.

- Take 10 minutes in the evenings to look over the next day's routine—or create one if you haven't—so that you don't feel unprepared or panicked in the morning.

9. Do Something You Enjoy

Can you remember the last time you were doing an activity that made you feel excited? How did you feel at that moment? One of the words you may use to describe your emotions is "energized." When you are doing something you are passionate about, time flies and you remain focused on the task at hand. Since you enjoy what you are doing, your mind is fully absorbed in the activity and for a brief moment, you forget about your worries and stressors.

Think about an activity that you can do at home that you absolutely love. It could be painting, baking, playing a sport, or building a DIY project. You don't need to come up with a list of things—just one really enjoyable activity will do! Each week, dedicate an hour of uninterrupted time to performing an activity you enjoy. Switch off your cell phone, isolate yourself in a room, and focus all of your attention on your activity.

10. Listen to Music

Music has the ability to lift your mood and improve depressive symptoms. It can help you get into a positive state of mind, reduce feelings of stress, and provide entertainment. In ancient traditions, particularly in the East, music has always been used for meditation. When the relaxing practice of meditation is coupled with calming music, it can lower stress and anxiety and increase your focus and energy levels.

If you are passionate about music, then you may benefit from music therapy. Unlike casually listening to music, music therapy allows you to have purposeful interactions with music through playing, composing, or listening to music. The goal-oriented musical activities can help you work through difficult emotions and feel a lot lighter and happier.

Certain music genres, such as classical or ambient music, have been found to reduce stress. However, all music genres (especially those you enjoy) are useful in lowering stress and boosting your moods. You might also assign significance to each genre, like playing rap music when you need motivation and playing rock music when you desire to develop your self-esteem.

11. Spend Time in Nature

Studies have shown that spending as little as 20 minutes in nature can help you build emotional resilience and increase positive feelings (Fabrega, 2014). Another study that observed over 300,000 Dutch participants' medical records found those who lived within a mile of a local park or any other green space experienced less anxiety and depression than those who lived farther away from a green space (Walters, 2011).

Besides how calming it is being around nature, getting exposure to natural sunlight comes with its benefits too. When the sun rays touch your skin, a process occurs where your body begins to generate vitamin D. Vitamin D is known to strengthen your bones, teeth, and muscles, as well as to improve your overall moods.

Spending time in nature doesn't have to be boring. Here is a list of fun nature activities you can try the next time you are outside:

- Take a nap on the grass

- Go camping with friends

- Jog around your neighborhood

- Ride a bicycle

- Watch the sunset

- Walk your dog

- Read a book under a tree

- Listen to a new music album while walking

- Start gardening or growing vegetables

- Have a picnic

- Visit a local farmer's market

In 2013, the David Suzuki Foundation created a 30X30 Nature Challenge where they challenged like many people as possible to spend 3o minutes in nature for 30 days. Those who participated in the challenge reported having more energy, feeling happier, and having fewer sleep disturbances after the 30-day challenge was over.

Are you up for the challenge? Can you spend 30 minutes outdoors, for 30 days?

12. Spend Time With Loved Ones

Spending time with close friends and family can offer you the emotional support you need while recovering from depression. Ideally, face-to-face interactions provide more opportunities to bond with your loved ones, however, if this isn't possible, you can use video and voice calls.

The relationship a teenager has with their parents has been found to impact their aspirations in life. For example, parents who spent quality time with their teenage children, bonding over books, cultural events, or family outings, were seen to raise their children's aspirations.

Spending time with loved ones doesn't need to feel like an extra chore. There are fun ways you can connect with your friends and family and make memories while doing so. Here are a few suggestions to get you inspired:

- Share the highs and lows of your day

- Prepare dinner together

- Solve a household problem together

- Plan your next family vacation

- Attend a fair or market

- Talk about your future goals

- Have a movie marathon

- Develop a healthy habit together (and hold each other accountable)

- Try out a new restaurant serving different cuisine

- Take a 30 challenge together

- Take a craft class together

13. Try Something New

When you are accustomed to following the same routines every day, the same parts of your brain light up, which limits how much information you can learn. Trying something new can be the solution to boredom or feeling stuck in life. The first step when trying something new is to brainstorm as many ideas as possible. Remember, there are no bad ideas, so have fun thinking outside the box or recalling experiences you have always wanted to try.

While brainstorming, you can also create lists of several things such as

- List of things you have always wanted to learn (eg. Language, creative skill, cooking, etc.)

- List of places you have always wanted to see (eg. Local museum, heritage site, a restaurant in your city, etc.)

- List of goals you have always wanted to accomplish (eg. Learn how to swim, lose weight or gain muscle, start your own YouTube channel, etc.)

The next step is to look at your ideas and lists and pick one thing that you will try first. Go for the first activity or goal that jumps out at you or makes you feel the most excited. Once you have picked an activity or goal, you can plan the execution. Conduct research about the subject and find out how other people succeeded at it. Search for advice on how to overcome obstacles that may come as you complete your activity or goal.

You can also look for practical information, such as how much a certain course costs, how long it takes to learn a language, or what kind of diet or fitness plan supports your weight loss journey. Put all of your information under one folder on your computer so you can easily access it whenever you need it. Finally, set S.M.A.R.T goals to manage time and measure your progress as you go along. When you have successfully attempted something new, go back to your brainstorming notes and pick another new thing to try!

14. Volunteer

Volunteering is rewarding because helping others feels good! Volunteers often experience what is known as the "helper's high" which is a feeling of calmness and satisfaction after doing something kind for another person. A lifestyle of helping others can further increase an individual's self-esteem and even provide them with a purpose in life. Moreover, volunteering is a social activity and can provide opportunities for meeting new people and being part of a community.

There are different types of volunteering available for you to choose from, including

- **Traditional volunteering:** Donating your money or spending time at a local charity. This type of volunteering can be done for a few hours over a weekend, or on an ongoing basis.

- **Gap year volunteering:** While deciding on your next career or educational move, you can take a year off and volunteer for a charity organization or go on a mission at church. This type of volunteering requires more commitment since it may involve relocating to another country for a year.

- **Voluntourism:** You can sign up with an agency or organization to travel the world, meet new people, and make a positive impact in the places you visit. Similar to gap year volunteering, you may be expected to leave your state or country for an extended period of time. It's crucial to conduct research before committing to an overseas opportunity to ensure it is a good fit for you and that you will be safe.

- **Online volunteering:** Since the Covid-19 era, online volunteering has grown in popularity. There are now more people seeking help from online tutors and mentors with learning skills. The upside of this type of volunteering is you don't need to leave the house, plus most opportunities pay an hourly rate.

There are a few questions to ask yourself when deciding on the best volunteering opportunity:

- Do I want to do something that requires my skills or talents?

- Do I want to volunteer in person or online?

- Am I looking for a once-off volunteering opportunity or something I can do on a recurring basis?

- Do I want to volunteer for an organization or a local shelter, church, or orphanage?

- Do I want to be paid for volunteering?

15. Practice Gratitude

You can manage your depressive symptoms by teaching yourself to recognize the goodness in your life. This is because, as mentioned in the previous chapter, gratitude can positively influence how you see yourself and your environment. Furthermore, making gratitude a daily practice by writing down a few things you are grateful for can help you feel more positive about your life.

Here is five days' worth of gratitude journal prompts that you can work on to make gratitude a daily practice:

Monday

- Write about one good thing that happened to you today.

- Write about your favorite hobby.

- Write about your pet (or pets you had when you were younger) and what makes them special.

Tuesday

- Write about something good that you saw someone else do.

- Remember a goal you achieved and write a thank you letter to the people who helped you achieve it (you can send them the letter if you would like, however, it's not mandatory).

- Write about a friend who has been a positive influence in your life.

Wednesday

- Write down something that made you smile today.

- Write about something that makes you proud of yourself.

- List at least five strengths you love about yourself.

Thursday

- Write about something interesting that happened in your life today.

- Write about the highlight of your day.

- Think back to one of your favorite childhood memories and write about what made that moment so special.

Friday

- Write about something you did well today.

- Write about something you are discovering about yourself. It could be a strength, personality trait, or preference that you are learning about yourself.

- Write about what uplifts your mood when you are feeling down.

Your responses to each prompt can be as long or short as you would like. After the week is over, read through your responses and take the time to reflect on how much goodness there is in your life. If you enjoy working with journal prompts, you can think of a few more of your own and continue the exercise independently.

16. Practice Meditation

Meditation is another self-regulation practice that we have already discussed in the previous chapter. The reason meditation is so effective in managing anxiety and depression is because it creates stillness in the mind, giving you an opportunity to break cycles of overthinking, negative self-talk, and simply enjoy being in the present moment. So often, when you are feeling depressed or anxious, your mind has wandered to the past or the future. Meditation gently brings your mind back to your present experience so you can focus on what you are feeling or thinking at the moment. Below is a short guided meditation that you can practice at home:

- Sit in a comfortable position against a wall or chair. You can also lie on your bed if that would make you feel most comfortable, although try not to fall asleep.

- If you are lying on your back, ensure the back of your body is touching the surface beneath you. If you are in a sitting position, straighten your back and relax your arms and shoulders.

- Gently close your eyes and focus on your breathing. First, notice the natural rhythm of your breath without trying to control it. Are you taking short and choppy breaths? Or slow and consistent breaths?

- Notice how your body is feeling. Do you sense any tension in your body? Do you have any aches and pains? Or are there recurring thoughts that are distracting you?

- Take three slow and deep breaths and then place one hand over your heart. Notice if doing this makes you feel anything different. Continue taking deep breaths and repeat the following phrases in your mind:

  o "I am enough"

  o "I am a loving person"

  o "I am kind"

  o "I deserve to be taken care of"

o "I deserve to be seen"

- Take 10 deep breaths. With each inhaled breath, draw as much love inside your body as you can. And with each exhale breath, release the negative thoughts or beliefs you have about yourself.

- Repeat the phrases to yourself again, this time saying them out loud. You can recite them as many times as you like, giving as much thought to each one. Here are the five phrases:

    o "I am enough"

    o "I am a loving person"

    o "I am kind"

    o "I deserve to be taken care of"

    o "I deserve to be seen"

- If your mind wanders at any point during the meditation, gently bring your focus back to the breathing. If you happen to have a negative thought, simply observe what it is and allow it to disappear naturally.

- When you are ready, take a few deep breaths and open your eyes. You can remain in your meditation position for a few more minutes and reflect on your experience.

17. Consider What You Eat

Similar to how there are anti-anxiety foods that reduce or protect you against feelings of anxiety, there are also anti-depression foods that work in a similar way. Nevertheless, there is no proven diet that can cure depression. Below are vital minerals, vitamins, and nutrients found in certain foods that can help you manage your depressive symptoms:

- Your brain needs antioxidants to fight against oxidative stress, which can cause depression and anxiety disorders. You can increase your intake of antioxidants by consuming certain foods, such as beta-carotene (found in broccoli, carrots, spinach, pumpkin, collards, etc.), vitamin C (found in blueberries, grapefruit, potatoes, oranges, etc.), and vitamin E (found in nuts and seeds, vegetable oils, wheat germ, etc.)

- Healthy carbohydrates, like whole grains and fresh whole fruits and vegetables, can increase the production of serotonin, the mood-boosting brain chemical. Refined, complex carbohydrates found in sugary processed foods don't have the same effect, so try to avoid these at all costs.

- If depression is negatively impacting your levels of concentration, add more protein-rich foods to your diet. Protein is known to increase alertness and boost your energy, and some proteins like chicken, turkey, or tuna contain tryptophan, an amino acid that helps your brain make serotonin. Other great sources of protein include beans, low-fat cheese, lean beef, soy products, and fish.

- Low selenium in the body has been linked to depression. Selenium is an essential mineral that supports a number of body functions, including your immune system and brain health. You can find selenium in foods like beans and legumes, low-fat dairy products, nuts, and seeds, as well as seafood.

- Not consuming enough omega-3 fatty acids has been linked with higher rates of major depressive disorder. Omega-3s are known to improve heart health and improve your overall mood. Great sources of omega-3 fatty acids include flaxseed, fatty fish, walnuts, leafy green vegetables, and canola oil.

Knowing which foods to consume to boost your mood, energy, and focus is a good place to start. However, on a daily basis, you will need to prepare meals that incorporate some of these foods. You may not be fortunate enough to have someone prepare nutritious meals for you, which leaves most of the prep work and meal planning on your shoulders.

Below are simple meal options that are easy enough to prepare on your own and don't require a lot of time in the kitchen:

Breakfast

- Whole-grain cereal with low-fat milk and blueberries

- Banana, almond, and flaxseed smoothie

- Low-fat Greek yogurt with honey and granola

- Avocado on toast

Lunch

- Peanut butter on wholewheat toast

- White bean soup with sauerkraut

- Salmon salad with vinaigrette

- Beet, citrus, and avocado salad

- Miso soup

Dinner

- Turkey burger with sweet potato fries

- Lentil and vegetable stew

- Seafood pasta

- Almond-crusted barramundi fish with brown rice

During the day, you can enjoy healthy snacks that won't spike your blood sugar levels and leave you feeling sluggish. Here are a few healthy snacks to consider:

- Chocolate granola bars

- Bag of mixed nuts

- Fresh fruit with yogurt

- Smoothies and healthy juices

18.

19. Take a Walk

There will be days when you don't feel like exerting too much energy through physical exercise. On days like these, you can still get up and move your body by taking a walk. This is considered low-intensity exercise and won't be strenuous on your body. There are so many benefits of walking, like improving blood circulation, lightening your mood, improving sleep, and giving you time to clear your mind. You can make your walks fun by walking with a friend, listening to music, playing a walking game on an app, or challenging yourself to walk more steps each day.

20. Get Enough Sleep

One of the most common symptoms of depression is sleep disturbance. This usually occurs when you have trouble falling asleep, experience interrupted sleep, or suffer from sleeping too little (known as insomnia) or sleeping too much (known as hypersomnia). The relationship between sleep and depression is a complex one. Getting too little sleep can eventually lead to depression, but having depression can lead to poor sleep.

When you don't get enough quality sleep, it can negatively affect the rest of your life. Your energy levels, moods, and concentration reach an all-time low, and it becomes difficult carrying out everyday tasks and routines. While quality sleep won't completely heal depression, it can help you manage depressive symptoms. Here are a few tips on how you can ensure you get quality sleep every night:

- Ensure you get between 7—9 hours of sleep per night.

- Follow your sleeping schedule.

- Make sure your bedroom is dark and quiet. If you live in a noisy house or next to a noisy street, get a pair of earplugs.

- Switch to a comfortable mattress and buy pillows that offer you the right kind of head and neck support.

- Create a no technology rule in your bedroom.

- Avoid drinking caffeinated drinks after lunchtime.

21. Consider Clinical Treatment

If all of these suggestions haven't helped you reduce your symptoms of depression, then you may benefit from speaking to a mental health specialist or therapist about your mental health. They have the necessary skills and tools to evaluate your physical and psychological condition and provide a tailored treatment plan. Since there are many different types of treatments for depression, finding the right one for you can take time. Be open to trying as many types of treatments as possible, so you can find the best option.

Key Takeaways

Depression is by nature a mental health condition that causes you to feel drained, lose interest in social activities, and feel unmotivated. It isn't possible to wake up one morning and not feel depressed because these symptoms affect how you think and feel about yourself and your life. Therefore, working through depressive symptoms takes a great deal of patience and consistent effort in stepping outside of your comfort zone and looking for different ways to boost your energy, uplift your moods, and increase positive feelings about yourself. There are many methods that you can try to help alleviate symptoms of depression. Try as many different options and see which works best for you. After getting your symptoms under control, the next step is to address the negative thoughts and beliefs that trigger stress and anxiety.

Chapter 7:

Say Goodbye to Negative

Thoughts

In this chapter, you will learn:

- How to stop negative thinking using a simple 5 step process.

- Identify and switch negative thoughts to positive ones.

What Is Negative Thinking?

It is normal to feel disappointed about your performance in a test or worry about future events from time to time. Like many other young people, you are exposed to so much disheartening information in the news and on social media that you can easily start to imagine the worst-case scenarios taking place in your life or community. However, when doubts and fears enter your mind on a daily basis, they can start to negatively impact your mental health.

Negative thinking is a pattern of thinking negatively about yourself and your environment. Since it is a pattern, you automatically see things from a negative point of view, rather than assess a situation for what it is worth. Your negative thinking patterns create negative assumptions and beliefs that justify your outlook on life. The reason negative thinking is so harmful is as it can cause you to adopt unrealistic and limiting beliefs about yourself or your environment that interfere with your quality of life.

Not everybody who engages in negative thinking suffers from a mental health condition. However, those who do think negatively are more vulnerable to mental health problems. In some cases, negative thinking can be a symptom of an existing mental health illness, such as generalized anxiety disorder, depression, or obsessive-compulsive disorder.

To get to the bottom of negative thinking, it's worth understanding what normally triggers it, to begin with. There are three main triggers of negative thinking, which are:

- Fear of the unknown and being uncertain of what the future will bring.

- Worrying about what other people think about you.

- Fear of losing control or being in an unpredictable situation.

- Regrets or guilt about past mistakes or failures.

- Experiencing a traumatic life event that changes your outlook on life.

- Losing support or being betrayed by a loved one.

- Comparing your appearance or position in life to someone else.

- Holding extremely high and unrealistic standards for your life.

- Developing an inferiority complex and thinking that life has been unfair to you.

When negative thoughts aren't recognized and addressed appropriately, they can turn into a habit. In other words, even when you are not aware of it, you might worry about everyday tasks and find it difficult to think rationally about things. The habit of negative thinking can also be spurred by the media, language, or information you are continuously exposed to.

For example, if you are following a pessimistic influencer on social media, watching their content on a daily basis might cause you to adopt the same pessimistic viewpoint and see your life in the same manner. Or if you find yourself drawn to negative news about current affairs, you might become obsessed with hearing about the negative things happening around the world, and soon you might start to think that the world is inherently dangerous.

The good news is that you can break the habit of negative thinking by simply learning to slow down your thought processes and challenge each thought. It is estimated that each person has about 5,000 spontaneous thoughts every day. Out of these 5,000 thoughts, the negative ones are likely to receive more attention. Instead of feeling guilty for thinking negatively, you can practice observing your negative thoughts and seeing them for what they are.

Five Steps to Eliminate Negative Thinking

Excessive negative thinking can lead to anxiety, depression, and a lowered self-esteem. The solution to addressing negative thinking is to recognize negative thoughts (and the consequences of negative thinking), then use strategies to adjust, change, or challenge these thoughts.

Below are five steps on how to recognize, challenge, and work through negative thoughts:

Step 1: Identify Negative Thoughts

Negative thoughts are normally caused by cognitive distortions, which are thought patterns that cause you to assess reality in an inaccurate way. In most cases, cognitive distortions are negative and make you view your life in a negative and distorted light. Here are a few examples of cognitive distortions to help you get an idea of what they sound like:

"I failed my math test. I am probably going to fail the grade."

"My friend hasn't responded to my text. I think they are upset with me."

"My plans didn't work out as I hoped. I am such a failure."

"I am single because I am ugly."

"My friend is running late. I hope they are not in danger."

It is not helpful to judge yourself for having cognitive distortions. Doing so only makes you feel worse. Instead of being cynical, you can view cognitive distortions as being errors in thinking. For example, you can respond to the thought of possibly failing the grade by saying to yourself "One math test won't cause me to fail the grade. I have several more opportunities to make up for it. I can do this!"

It's also useful to understand where cognitive distortions come from. Cognitive distortions are rooted in thoughts or beliefs that were developed during a difficult time. These distorted views about life may have helped you feel safe or make sense of the stressful situation you were going through. For example, a child who is reprimanded for expressing their emotions might grow up thinking that being open about feelings is wrong or unacceptable. While this belief could have made living at home feel safer, they may grow up with poor emotional regulation skills and struggle to form healthy relationships with others as a young adult.

There are several types of cognitive distortions, which we have already covered in the previous section. To summarize, these include

- All-or-nothing thinking

- Overgeneralization.

- Mental filtering

- Jumping to conclusions

- Emotional reasoning

- Labeling

Fortunately, these cognitive distortions can be corrected over time by taking certain steps:

- **Identify the cognitive distortion.** When you are able to recognize a negative thought, you have won half of the battle. This is because you are able to identify the thought which caused your mood to shift and where that thought possibly comes from.

- **Reframe the situation.** Drop the all-or-nothing thinking and step back from the situation to see other perspectives. Ask yourself: If a friend of mine had this thought, what would I think about it? Look for alternative interpretations of the situation so you can formulate different ideas and opinions (hopefully more positive).

- **Conduct a cost-benefit analysis.** Look at your thoughts and assess whether it is helpful or harmful to your mental and emotional well-being. Ask yourself whether or not the thought supports recovery and a healthy lifestyle. If a thought limits your quality of life, makes you afraid of taking risks, or causes you to doubt your own abilities, then it is a thought worth changing.

Below is an exercise that can help you fact-check every thought that comes to mind. Remember, thoughts don't necessarily represent what is true. You need to scrutinize each thought and determine whether it contains facts or if it is based on emotion or opinion. Look at each phrase in the first column of the table and relate it to your life, then place across if you believe it is based on facts, emotions, or an opinion about yourself.

Statement	Facts	Emotions	Opinions
Eg. "I'm weird"			X
"I'm not doing well at school"			
"I don't have friends"			
"My life is stressful"			
"I need to lose weight"			

Statement	Facts	Emotions	Opinions
"I'm not good enough"			
"I'm single"			
"I will be single forever"			
"I'm a disappointment to my family"			

Step 2: Replace Negative Thoughts

It is a lot easier to replace a negative thought after you have identified it. However, the process isn't as straightforward as you might think. There is still a part of your mind that believes the negative thought to be true. You need to wrestle with this part of your mind and provide as much evidence as you can that the thought isn't true. Unless you provide enough evidence disproving your negative thoughts, it may be difficult to eliminate it.

Cognitive restructuring is a psychological process that involves challenging your thoughts and exploring alternatives. It gives you the power to separate yourself from the thought and look at it objectively to see whether or not it is realistic and helpful. Here are a few steps you can take to practice cognitive restructuring:

- Ask yourself if the thought is realistic.

- Think back on the past when you were in a similar situation and assess whether your current thought matches the gravity of the situation. In other words, is your thought justified or is it an overreaction?

- Deliberately look for alternative explanations that are more positive or can help you overcome the situation you are in.

- Conduct a cost-benefit analysis and think about what you would gain or lose if you continued to entertain this thought.

- Determine whether your thought is a result of one of the different types of cognitive distortions.

- Consider the advice you would give a friend if they were in the same position as you.

Another way of replacing negative thoughts is to change a BLUE thought into a TRUE thought. As described by Amy Morin, a BLUE thought is an acronym that describes thoughts that encourage blaming, looking for bad news, unhappy guessing (making negative predictions about the future), and exaggerated negative thoughts (Morin, 2018). In comparison, a TRUE thought focuses on the truth and taking action. Unlike a BLUE thought, it is grounded in whatever is taking place now or has taken place in the past. They also lean toward the positive aspects of a situation, rather than focusing on the negative aspects.

All you need to do to replace a BLUE thought with a TRUE thought is to ask yourself: What advice would I give a loved one who had a similar problem? Naturally, since you care for your loved one, your advice would be practical and action-driven. You would encourage them to look at the positive aspects of the situation so they can overcome the difficulty.

For example, you would replace a thought like "I am a failure" with "I am not defined by my setbacks. I will succeed if I keep trying." Or replace a thought like "I will never get an A for this subject" with "If I continue taking notes in classes and attending tutoring classes, I will improve my grade."

Now it's your turn. Complete the column on the right by writing down TRUE thoughts to replace the BLUE thoughts in the left column:

BLUE Thought	TRUE Thought
Eg. "I am dumb"	"I am smart in my own way. I don't need to measure my intelligence with other people."
"I won't get accepted into college"	
"I can't make friends"	
"I will always be the odd one out"	
"I always say the wrong things"	
"I'm not as sociable as other kids"	
"I probably won't succeed in life"	

Step 3: Avoid Thought Stopping

Thought stopping is the act of immediately pushing down or rejecting a negative thought as soon as it comes to mind. This is an inappropriate way of replacing a negative thought. When you stop a negative thought, you aren't working through it, which means that it is likely to pop up again in your mind at some point or another.

Thought stopping also causes you to judge thought and label it as being "bad," "embarrassing," or "unacceptable." When you label a thought in this manner, you are indirectly passing judgment on yourself. In other words, since you entertained a "bad thought," you must be a "bad person." Of course, this isn't true, but the more you judge and label your negative thoughts, the harder it becomes to separate who you are from what you think.

To avoid thought stopping, learn to become more accepting of negative thoughts. Understand that your negative thoughts are rooted in cognitive distortions and therefore are not a fair representation of what's real. Accept your distorted thoughts for what they are without feeling ashamed or guilty for thinking in that way. Tell yourself: Just because I have a distorted thought, doesn't mean that I am distorted. The more you accept your negative thoughts, the less likely you will be anxious when you think about something dark, unkind, or exaggeratedly negative.

Step 4: Practice Coping With Criticism

It isn't realistic to think that people are always going to respond in a positive way toward you. Since you cannot control how another person perceives you, it is important to learn how to protect yourself against criticism or judgment from others. One way to do this is to develop your assertive responses to criticism. For example, you can look at a mirror and pretend that you are speaking to somebody who has criticized you. Depending on what the criticism is, you can recite one of the statements you have carefully prepared in response to criticism. You can also prepare general phrases to communicate how uncomfortable you are in triggering situations, like being forced to speak amongst a group of people.

Before we go into strategies on how to cope with criticism, it's important to mention that not all criticism is negative. There are generally two types of criticism you might receive from people. The first is constructive criticism, where you receive genuine feedback intended to help you grow or perform better. Constructive criticism is usually true in the sense that it is based on facts. For example, a teacher might say to you "I enjoyed reading your essay, but you still need to work on your grammar."

The second type of criticism is destructive criticism that is either not true (based on facts) or may be true but is said in a way that seeks to bring you down. Destructive criticism is inconsiderate of another person's feelings and can be used to shame, judge, or embarrass someone. For example, instead of telling you what errors to fix in your writing, a teacher might say "This essay is appalling! It sounds like a fifth-grader wrote it." After hearing a statement like that you may feel offended and think negatively about your abilities to write.

How you receive criticism has a lot to do with the kind of criticism you received as a child. If you were brought up receiving constructive criticism, then you might respond well to feedback or be corrected by others. However, if you were brought up receiving destructive criticism, then you might interpret any kind of criticism (even constructive criticism) as being a personal attack on you, or a form of rejection. Furthermore, receiving destructive criticism as a child can also teach you non-assertive strategies for responding to criticism such as:

- Walking away

- Shutting down

- Getting angry

- Being defensive

- Feeling confused

- Pretending you didn't hear it

- Pretending it didn't affect you

None of these strategies help you cope with criticism in a healthy way.

How you cope with criticism can also be linked to how you are as a person. If you are a passive person who generally avoids conflict, you may internalize your feelings and put on a brave face, acting as though nothing happened. Alternatively, you may agree with the criticism, even if it isn't true, and instead blame yourself. For example, if someone insults you for no valid reason, you might agree with the criticism and blame yourself for not being good enough. You might think, "That person is right. I am a loser and I need to get my life together."

If you have an aggressive personality, hearing criticism of any kind could make you become defensive. Even when the criticism is revealing a blind spot or helping you improve on your work, it feels as though you are being personally attacked. You might respond by saying, "How dare you think I am a loser. Have you seen yourself?" In most cases, aggressive responses like these lead to conflict and can still negatively affect your self-esteem.

Assertive people generally respond in the most effective way to criticism. They are able to distinguish between constructive and destructive criticism and respond to both appropriately. Furthermore, assertive people have the ability to separate what other people say or think about them from who they are as individuals. For example, they might respond to criticism by saying "You may think I am a loser, but that is your opinion, not a fact about who I am." What makes assertive responses effective is how well they communicate the truth while staying calm.

The good news is that you don't need to be an assertive person to learn how to respond to criticism in an assertive manner. Here are a few strategies on how to respond to both constructive and destructive criticism assertively:

1. Assertively Responding to Constructive Criticism

Remember that constructive criticism is designed to help you become a better person. It is said with good intentions, and if communicated properly, can be helpful. Here are a few strategies for responding to constructive criticism:

- If you believe the criticism is valid, accept it without displaying negative emotions. See the value in receiving feedback and thank the person for helping you improve on your skill.

- If someone exposes one of your negative qualities that are true, calmly agree with the criticism without apologizing or becoming defensive. Remind yourself that you are not perfect and thus, being shown your own weaknesses isn't a personal attack.

- If you are not convinced that the criticism is true, ask more questions so you can understand what the person meant by their criticism. For example, you might say "In what ways do you think I'm rude?" If the explanation is valid (backed up with evidence and examples), then you need to accept the criticism and thank the person for revealing a weakness you were not aware of. Once again, try not to see it as a personal attack if in fact what they are saying is true, and it was said in a respectful way.

2. Assertively Responding to Destructive Criticism

Destructive criticism can either be completely false, or it can be true but said in a manipulative or mean-spirited way. Even if destructive criticism is true, you do not deserve to be spoken down to by another person. Here are a few strategies on how to respond to destructive criticism:

- Disagree with false criticism in a calm way, and watch that you do not become passive or aggressive. For example, if someone says "You are so lazy" you can say "No, that's not true. I am not lazy. I may take my time to do things, but I am not lazy."

- There are times when you won't be sure whether the criticism is constructive or destructive. For example, it might have some truth to it but is communicated in a condescending way. It is better to ask for more details and understand what the person meant, rather than reacting with negative emotions.

- If there is some truth to destructive criticism, but it isn't completely valid, you can agree in part, agree in probability, or agree in principle. When you agree in part, you find a piece of the criticism that is true and disagree with the rest. When you agree on probability, you mention how something "may be possible" or "may be true." Lastly, when you agree in principle you acknowledge the person's logic without agreeing with their statement.

Step 5: Use a Thought Diary

A thought diary is a structured type of journal typically used in CBT. Unlike a traditional journal where you can write about anything you feel like, a thought diary is specifically used to record recurring thoughts, triggers, and behaviors to situations that occur in your life.

Using a thought diary can help you work through negative thoughts and understand what triggers them. For example, you might notice that each time you are around a certain group of people, you feel self-conscious. By recognizing this pattern, you can either replace your self-critical thoughts or distance yourself from that particular group of people.

The general structure of a thought diary requires you to record information in a table format. When creating your table, all you will need is four columns (although you can add more columns if you want to record more details about a situation). The four columns are:

Column 1: Situation

Column 2: Date when it happened

Column 3: Emotion and rating of emotional intensity

Column 4: Thought and rating of the strength of thought

Situation	Date	Emotion and rating	Thought and rating

When completing an entry in your thought diary, think back to a situation that you found overwhelming, then answer the following questions:

- What happened? (Column 1)

- When did it happen? (Column 2)

- What emotions did you experience, and how strong were these emotions on a scale of 1—10, 1 being very weak and 10 being extremely strong? (Column 3)

- What thoughts or beliefs were racing through your mind? How strong were these thoughts or beliefs on a scale of 1—10, 1 being very weak and 10 being extremely strong? (Column 4)

Your entry will look like this:

Situation	Date	Emotion and rating	Thought and rating
Trying to study for a test but having difficulty concentrating due to thinking I am going to fail the test.	02/02/2022	Anxious — 7/10 Irritable — 8/10	"I always disappoint myself" — 8.5/10

After recording an event in your thought diary, you can take it a step further and challenge your negative thoughts. There are a few ways you can challenge your thoughts:

- You can consider the evidence *against* the negative thought by looking at the rating and asking yourself if the thought was a cognitive distortion or in fact valid.

- Look for alternative ways of understanding the situation. Ask yourself, "Is there something I'm not seeing about this situation?"

- Consider the worst-case scenario and consider what might happen if you were to believe your overwhelming thought. Ask yourself, "What would be the consequences of believing this thought?"

After trying various strategies to challenge your negative thoughts, assess whether your thoughts have changed and re-rate the intensity of your emotions and thoughts in your thought diary.

Exercise: Cognitive Restructuring 101

Along with the other exercises in this chapter, this complete will help you break down your thought processes and restructure your thinking patterns. Record your thoughts in three columns. In the first column, write down a negative thought you are thinking. In the second column, provide information that either supports or disproves your thought. In the last column, state whether the thought is based on evidence or opinion.

What I'm Thinking	Facts For/Against the Thought	Is the Thought Based on Evidence or Opinion?

After completing the table, you can go one step further again and challenge your negative thought. Remember, the more you question a negative thought, the less believable it becomes. This is a good thing because it means your mind is learning how to look at reality in a true and realistic way. Here are a few more questions you can ask to challenge your negative thought:

- Are you using all-or-nothing thinking, or trying to simplify a matter that is complex in nature?

- Are you making any unverified assumptions that are causing you to misinterpret the situation?

- Do other people have different perspectives on the situation? If so, have you explored these alternative perspectives?

- Have you considered all of the facts, or are you looking at those which support your argument?

- Is it possible that you might be exaggerating reality?

- Are you entertaining the negative thought out of habit or because it is valid?

- Was this negative thought influenced by what you have heard from someone else? If so, do you believe they are a reliable source of truth?

Key Takeaways

When a negative thought takes over your mind, it can change how you look at yourself and the environment. It may cause you to doubt your abilities or make unverified assumptions about others. The guilt and shame that often follows after you have entertained a negative thought can make you pass blame or judgment on yourself. This creates a vicious cycle where your negative thoughts make you feel worse about who you are and the kind of lifestyle you live. The truth is that negative thoughts aren't bad. They are simply cognitive distortions that alter how you view reality.

You can change these distortions by first recognizing them and then learning different ways of challenging them. Replacing negative thoughts takes a lot of patience, however, with the exercises you have been given in this chapter, you have the necessary skills to restructure how you think. Once you can control negative thoughts, the final step in managing anxiety and depression is to look for ways to reduce stress.

Chapter 8:

Stress Test

In this chapter, you will learn:

- How to take the stress test so you can figure out your stress levels.

- Common stress triggers and how to manage external stressors (if possible).

- 10 Simple ways to relieve stress.

Taking the Stress Test

Below is a questionnaire that measures the degree to which you find certain life events stressful (Cohen, 1994). These questions will assess how overwhelming, unpredictable, and uncontrollable you find your life. Answer each question by reflecting on the thoughts and feelings you have felt during the last month. At the end, calculate your score and figure out your results.

Questions:

1. **How often have you been disappointed due to something that happened unexpectedly?**

    a. Never

    b. Almost never

    c. Sometimes

    d. Fairly often

    e. Very often

2. **How often do you feel like you are not in control of the events that occur in your life?**

    a. Never

    b. Almost never

    c. Sometimes

    d. Fairly often

    e. Very often

3. **How often have you felt stressed out or nervous?**

   a. Never

   b. Almost never

   c. Sometimes

   d. Fairly often

   e. Very often

4. **How often have you felt positive about your ability to solve problems that may come your way?**

   a. Never

   b. Almost never

   c. Sometimes

   d. Fairly often

   e. Very often

5. **How often have you felt things were moving in the right direction?**

   a. Never

   b. Almost never

   c. Sometimes

   d. Fairly often

   e. Very often

6. How often have you felt overwhelmed with the amount of responsibility on your shoulders?

   a. Never

   b. Almost never

   c. Sometimes

   d. Fairly often

   e. Very often

7. How often have you been able to cope with irritations on a daily basis?

   a. Never

   b. Almost never

   c. Sometimes

   d. Fairly often

   e. Very often

8. How often have you felt in control of things?

   a. Never

   b. Almost never

   c. Sometimes

   d. Fairly often

   e. Very often

9. **How often have you felt angry because of things outside of your control?**

    a. Never

    b. Almost never

    c. Sometimes

    d. Fairly often

    e. Very often

10. **How often have you felt like tasks or problems are piling up and becoming too much to deal with?**

    a. Never

    b. Almost never

    c. Sometimes

    d. Fairly often

    e. Very often

Here are the steps to calculate your score:

- Each question is worth a certain amount of points, such as:

Never = 0 points

Almost never = 1 point

Sometimes = 2 points

Fairly often = 3 points

Very often = 4 points

- The exceptions are questions 4, 5, 7, and 8. For these questions, reverse the point system like this:

Never = 4 points

Almost never = 3 points

Sometimes = 2 points

Fairly often = 1 point

Very often = 0 points

- Add up your scores for each question to get a grand total.

- Your grand total will be a number between 0 and 40. A score closer to 0 represents low levels of perceived stress, whereas a score closer to 40 represents higher levels of perceived stress. For example;

Scores between 0—13 represent low stress levels.

Scores between 14—26 represent moderate stress levels.

Scores between 27—40 represent high stress levels.

It's important to remember that this test works out your perceived stress levels, meaning how stressed you believe that you are. Your perception of how stressed you are can influence how stressful you find a situation in life. This proves that it isn't always the life event that causes the most stress in your life, but how stressful you perceive the life event to be. Therefore, learning how to challenge your perception of life circumstances can lower your stress levels.

This stress test should not be taken too seriously as it cannot be a 100% accurate way of measuring stress. Nonetheless, you can use it as a guide to figure out how urgent your need is to reduce your stress levels.

What Are Your Stress Triggers?

According to data collected by the American Psychological Association, the amount of stress experienced by teenagers is far greater than that of adults (Smith, 2016). In the association's Stress in America Survey, teens reported that school (83%), getting accepted into a good college or deciding what to do after high school (69%), and family finances (65%) were the most common sources of stress. As a result of being under so much stress, teens reported experiencing sleep problems, overeating or eating too little, and feeling anxious and irritable.

Stress in and of itself isn't dangerous. When it is detected in time and properly managed, it doesn't cause significant harm in a young person's life. However, when left undetected and poorly treated, stress can interfere with a teen's learning, relationships, and self-perception (how they look at themselves).

The best time to fight against stress is at the onset. In most cases, you will notice physical or emotional signs of being stressed. These signs often come when you are feeling triggered by a thought, emotion, or event taking place in your environment. Here are a few signs to be aware of that could indicate you are feeling stressed:

- Feeling agitated or on edge

- Getting sick more than usual

- Complaining about frequent headaches or stomach pains

- Changes in sleeping patterns or eating behaviors

- Avoiding regular daily activities

- Increased forgetfulness and experiencing trouble concentrating

These common signs of stress are often triggered by something. As mentioned above, the common stressors for teens are related to school, plans after high school, and family financial matters. However, there are other potential triggers that may be the source of stress. Here are a few factors to consider:

- **Social stress.** Young people place significant importance on their social lives. The absence of peer support or peer acceptance can trigger stress. Other stress triggers include bullying, name-calling or being criticized, conflict in romantic relationships, and peer pressure.

- **Family issues.** Besides financial instability at home, teens may also be stressed by dysfunctional family dynamics, such as having a parent who is an alcoholic or who suffers from a chronic illness. Other stress triggers include witnessing parents' marital problems, sibling rivalry, and bullying, or strained relationships with parents.

- **Unpredictable world events.** Societal and political discord can also cause teens severe stress. For instance, hearing about a school shooting, natural disasters, or a global pandemic can create a lot of anxiety. Furthermore, since teenagers have access to the media, they can misinterpret what they read or believe false news that could make them question their sense of safety.

- **Traumatic events.** Being directly or indirectly affected by abuse, violence, or grief can be stressful for a young person. Unlike an adult, they may not have the psychological tools to make sense of and heal from the death of a loved one, a tragic accident, or being a victim of abuse. As a result, this makes young people vulnerable to experiencing post-traumatic stress disorder (PTSD) in the aftermath of trauma.

- **Major life changes.** Change can be difficult to accept for anyone, especially a teenager who thrives on stability and consistency. When a young person experiences major life changes like witnessing their parents getting a divorce, relocating to another country, or changing schools, it can make them feel confused and overwhelmed.

Exercise: Recognizing and Protecting Yourself Against Stress

There are many different factors that can cause you to become stressed. Learning to recognize when your stress response has been triggered gives you the chance to act before the stress takes over your body. Below is an exercise that will help you recognize the effects of stress on your mind and body and strengthen your protective measures against stress.

The table below has three columns. Under each column write down how stress impacts you on a physical, emotional, and behavioral level.

Physical Effects	Emotional Effects	Behavioral Effects

From each column, identify the most troubling ways that stress affects you. Next, focus on the protective factors that are within your control, which can improve the way you cope with the impact of stress. Below are six types of protective factors. Consider each one and how it can help you manage the impact of stress on your life.

Social support

- The ability to talk to someone about your problems.

- Being able to ask for help when you need it.

- Feeling loved and supported by close friends and family.

Physical health

- Getting sufficient physical exercise each week.

- Eating a nutrient-rich and balanced diet.

- Taking medication as prescribed by your doctor.

Self-esteem

- Believing that you are a valuable person and have something to offer the world.

- Accepting your personal strengths and weaknesses.

- Learning from your mistakes and celebrating your successes.

- Believing in your ability to overcome obstacles in life.

Coping skills

- The ability to regulate your emotions and remain calm in challenging situations.

- Be aware of your behaviors and how they affect others.

- Knowing how to self-soothe and relax your mind and body.

- Being able to express your thoughts and emotions and draw healthy boundaries.

Sense of purpose

- Finding meaning in what you are studying.

- Feeling a sense of belonging in your family, friendship group, or community.

- Creating personal values and living your life according to those values.

Healthy thinking

- The ability to identify negative thoughts and not dwell on them.

- Having an optimistic outlook on life.

- The ability to see the benefits or positive aspects of an unfavorable situation.

- Feeling a sense of gratitude for who you are and the life you live.

After considering each protective factor, you may find that there are some you still need to develop. Write these ones down, along with a few strategies on how you can develop them. You can even create short or long-term goals related to the protective factors you seek to improve on.

Ten Ways to Relieve Stress

Unfortunately, stress is one of those factors that will come and go as you experience life transitions, crises, or unexpected life situations. The presence of stress in your life doesn't need to make you feel anxious, especially if you are aware of your stress triggers and have a stress management toolkit to help you cope with stress.

Different coping strategies work for different people. Your goal should be to find the tools and activities that are effective in reducing your levels of stress. Below are 10 suggestions for coping strategies that can help you manage your stress levels:

1. Get More Active

Physical exercise is a great way to manage stress and clear your mind, however, it's only effective when it is done on a regular basis. The benefit of exercise is that there are so many variations and levels of intensity, so you can find the best workouts or physical activities that suit your lifestyle.

2. Follow a Balanced Diet

As mentioned in previous chapters, a healthy and balanced diet can reduce symptoms of anxiety and depression. Moreover, a healthy diet regulates how much sugar you consume, which can help to lower stress and manage your moods.

3. Put Limits on Your Technology Usage

Since you are old enough to set limits on how much media you consume, ensure the rules you set to promote a healthy and stress-free lifestyle. You can dedicate special days during the week where you check your social media and set a time limit for how long you spend online. For example, if you enjoy going on YouTube, you can make Fridays your YouTube day and block out 2-5 hours of watching YouTube videos. This will ensure your time spent online is used constructively and your media consumption doesn't affect other areas of your life, such as your school or personal relationships.

4. Consider Taking Supplements

If you have any vitamin or mineral deficiencies, taking natural supplements can regulate your body's stress response, brain health, moods, and overall functioning. Alternatively, you can take supplements that actively work to reduce stress, such as magnesium, ashwagandha, B vitamins, or L-theanine supplements.

5. Practice Self-Care

Self-care is the quality time you spend alone doing things that uplift your mood and improve your physical, mental, and emotional well-being. What feels uplifting to one person won't necessarily have the same effects on someone else, therefore when creating a self-care routine focus on the things that spark desire, passion, and excitement in you. Here are a few examples of self-care practices:

- Take a bath

- Declutter your room

- Play with your pet

- Bake a cake

- Call a friend

- Practice a hobby

- Read a book

Making time for at least one self-care practice a week can lower your stress levels and inject some much needed excitement in your life!

6. Reduce Caffeine Intake

Caffeine is a chemical typically found in energy drinks, coffee, and tea. When consumed, caffeine activates your nervous system and triggers a feeling of alertness. Although, many times, this feeling of alertness is accompanied by jitters, heart palpitations, and feelings of anxiety. When consumed in excess, caffeine can also interrupt normal sleep and wake cycles and leave you feeling exhausted and irritable. If you cannot imagine cutting out caffeine completely, commit to a single cup of coffee or tea in the morning. Otherwise, switch to decaffeinated beverages, herbal teas, and good ol' fashioned water.

7. Make Time for Friends and Family

A great stress reliever is being around people who love you. Just having a simple discussion or catch-up session can uplift your mood and relax your mind. If you don't have a social support network, perhaps this is the perfect time to reach out to close friends and family and invest more of your time in a few meaningful relationships. Alternatively, you can join a sports team, social club, or volunteering group and connect with others within your community.

8. Learn to Say No

Healthy relationships are built on healthy boundaries. When you feel respected and safe in a person's company, you are more likely to be relaxed and open up about your thoughts and feelings. To feel respected and safe in relationships, you need to learn when to draw the line and say no to requests, favors, or added responsibilities that drain your energy. While it's good to be generous with your time, money, and energy, it is also good to know when you are running on empty and need to reinvest time into taking care of yourself. Here are a few types of boundaries you can set to protect yourself:

- **Intellectual boundaries:** Setting boundaries to protect your thoughts, beliefs, and opinions. Remind yourself every day that you are entitled to think differently than other people.

- **Emotional boundaries:** Setting boundaries to protect how you feel about any given situation. Remind yourself on a daily basis that all of your emotions are valid and deserve to be felt, understood, and expressed.

- **Physical boundaries:** Setting boundaries to protect your physical space and privacy. Remind yourself every day that you are entitled to privacy and spend as much time as you need alone.

- **Social boundaries:** Setting boundaries to regulate your social interactions. Remind yourself often that your social needs are unique and you don't need to have the same social preferences as other people to have fun and feel satisfied in your relationships.

Saying no feels uncomfortable the first few times, but eventually, it enables you to set healthy boundaries and avoid putting yourself in awkward or uncomfortable situations. Your "No" can be a lifesaver, particularly in relationships with people who are negative or add stress to your life in some way. Write down examples of scenarios where you draw the line and practice saying these statements while looking into a mirror.

9. Avoid Procrastination

Another great way to relieve stress is to learn to reduce your task load and have fewer priorities. This will reduce the likelihood of procrastination or feeling overwhelmed with the amount of responsibility in your life. A great technique to practice when managing your daily tasks is the 80/20 rule. The

80/20 rule states that only 20% of your tasks bring 80% of value. In other words, if you had 10 tasks to complete in a day, only 2 of them would take priority. Every morning, write down a list of tasks you need to perform. Then, look at each task and ask yourself if it is part of the 20% that brings in 80% of the value. Prioritize the 20% and don't feel bad if you don't get around to completing the other tasks.

10. Spend Time With Your Pet

If you are fortunate enough to have a pet, this last strategy applies to you! Studies have found that pets can help humans lower stress and improve overall moods. This is because when you cuddle your furry animal, your brain releases oxytocin which is a bonding chemical that can lower your heart rate and blood pressure, as well as reduce feelings of loneliness. Spending time with your pet can give you a sense of purpose and motivate you to try out new activities like walking, spending time outdoors, or practicing speaking to someone about your feelings (your pet is the best listener!)

Exercise: Creating Your Stress Management Plan

Now that you have learned about common stress triggers, protective factors that can help you cope with recurring stressful events, and some tips on how to relieve stress, you have all of the information required to put together a stress management plan. For this final exercise, you will need a big sheet of paper or a journal. Your stress management plan can be designed as a table, mind map, collage of pictures, or any other creative representation you can think of!

To start, you will need to divide the stress management plan into four sections:

Section 1: How to Tackle the Problem

Section 2: How to Take Care of My Body

Section 3: How to Deal With Emotions

Section 4: How to Give Back to Others

The point of the plan is to come up with as many ideas and strategies on how to cope with stress in the healthiest ways possible. Avoid overthinking or judging your ideas. Simply write down whatever comes to mind. You don't need to try out every idea either, however, the more options you have written down, the greater your selection of choice will be when faced with a stressful situation.

Below are a few ideas and strategies that you can incorporate into your stress management plan. Feel free to add to these ideas or personalize each one according to your values, personality, or preferences.

Section 1: How to Tackle the Problem

The first section consists of ideas on how to identify triggers, assess whether there is a real or perceived problem, and de-escalating the situation.

- Write down what is happening and how it is making you feel.

- Step out of your shoes and look at the situation from an observer's perspective. Now, write down what is happening from a different perspective.

- Practice relaxation techniques like breathing exercises, meditation, or journaling to calm your mind and body.

- If you are unclear about how to solve a problem, break it down into small tasks or steps.

- If you don't think you can solve the problem on your own, ask for help (create a list of people you can contact when faced with different types of problems).

- Identify the people, places, or things that trigger stress and avoid them at all costs.

Section 2: How to Take Care of My Body

The second section consists of ideas on how to practice physical self-care and set healthy boundaries that protect your space and sense of safety.

- Make physical exercise a healthy habit.

- Ensure you are getting sufficient rest (at least 7—9 hours of sleep every night).

- Eat a diet that helps you maintain energy throughout the day and regulate your moods.

- Learn to say no when you are feeling overworked or have overcommitted yourself to plans.

Section 3: How to Deal With Emotions

The third section consists of ideas to help you regulate your emotions, manage your negative thoughts, and regain a sense of control over how you behave in any given situation.

- Reframe a negative situation so you can see the positive aspects of it.

- Learn how to respond assertively to criticism without showing negative emotions.

- When you have a thought, take a moment to pause and remind yourself that thoughts are not necessarily an indication of reality. Some thoughts are based on emotion and others on opinion or cognitive distortions.

- Spend time on activities that make you feel good about life.

- Find at least three people you trust to share your thoughts and emotions.

- Make journaling a daily practice.

- Make gratitude a daily practice.

- Accept the things that make you unique.

Section 4: How to Give Back to Others

The last section offers ideas on how you can give back to your loved ones and community to add value to those around you. When you feel as though you are making a positive contribution to the lives of others, you can experience a greater sense of satisfaction and purpose in your life.

- Spend quality time with your family

- Schedule a catch-up call with your close friends or cousins.

- Volunteer your time or skills at a local charity.

Key Takeaways

While you cannot control the kind of life stressors you are exposed to, you can control how you respond to stressful events. It's not selfish to say no, draw boundaries, or take some time for yourself when you are feeling stressed. When you are overwhelmed, your physical, emotional, and mental well-being should take priority. Identifying your stress triggers is the first step to coping with stress. Thereafter, you will be able to select the best coping strategies to turn to. Go ahead and try out some of the coping strategies and exercises suggested throughout the book, so you can better the most effective methods, tools, and coping skills that work for you.

Conclusion

We cannot deny that life is a lot more stressful today than it was several decades ago. There are many social, economic, and political factors that trigger anxiety—not to mention abuse, strained relationships, and family problems that completely drain what remains of our energy.

Unlike adults who have the advantage of life experience, teens are forced to deal with these pressures and triggers without having learned the necessary psychological tools or coping strategies. It is only through information books like these that teens get to understand what their problems are, where they come from, and how to respond to them in a healthy way.

Anxiety and depression are perhaps two of the most prevalent types of mental health conditions. They affect people of all races, ages, genders, social classes, and cultures. Thanks to celebrities like Selena Gomez and Justin Bieber, young people are able to recognize that they are not the only ones battling mental illness—they are millions of people similar to them who are also looking for ways to improve their mental health.

Even though many young people can relate to experiencing anxiety and depression, these conditions usually affect individuals in very different ways. It's therefore useful to learn about your specific symptoms and get a personal diagnosis from a doctor. This will allow you to treat your anxiety or depression according to your personality, lifestyle choices, and preferences.

There is no cure for anxiety or depression because these are natural conditions that arise in response to stressful events. Nonetheless, there are a variety of treatment options available to manage the symptoms of anxiety and depression so that they don't interfere with your quality of life. Once again, choosing the right treatment option is about finding a therapy, medication, or healthy lifestyle habit that matches your lifestyle needs.

To complement your treatment plan, you can refer to the tools, strategies, and exercises provided in this book. These resources, backed by CBT, are intended to help you identify and work through your thoughts and emotions so you can increase your self-esteem, turn off the stress response in your body, and respond to life events in a productive and positive way.

If you have found this book informative, please leave a review.

About the Author

Richard Bass is a well-established author with extensive knowledge and background on children's disabilities. Richard has also experienced first-hand many children and teens who deal with depression and anxiety. He enjoys researching techniques and ideas to better serve students, as well as providing guidance to parents on how to understand and lead their children to success.

Richard Bass holds a bachelor's and master's degree in education as well as several certifications including Special Education K-12, and Educational Administration.

He wants to share his experience, research, and practices through his writing, as it has proven successful to many parents and students.

Richard feels there is a need for parents and others around the child to fully understand the disability, he hopes that with his writing people will be more understanding of children with disabilities. He hopes his writing also helps teens with anxiety and depression to overcome it or help others overcome it.

Whenever Richard is not working, reading, or writing he likes to travel with his family to learn about different cultures as well as get ideas from all around the world about the upbringing of children, especially those with disabilities. Richard also researches and learns about different educational systems around the world.

Richard participates in several online groups where parents, educators, doctors, and psychologists share their success with children with disabilities. He plans to form a group where further discussion about his books and techniques could take place. Apart from online groups, he has also attended training regarding the upbringing of students with disabilities and has also led training in this area.

Richard has published two other books apart from this one including A Beginner's Guide on Parenting Children with ADHD and Parenting Children with Oppositional Defiant Disorder.

If you have any questions, feel free to contact Richard at richiebass27@outlook.com

A Message From the Author

If you enjoyed the book and are interested in further updates or just a place to share your thoughts with other readers or myself, please join my Facebook group by scanning below!

If you would be interested in receiving a FREE Planner for kids PDF version, by signing up you will also receive exclusive notifications when new content is released and will be able to receive it at a promotional price. Scan below to sign up!

References

3 Ways to practice gratitude (for teens). (n.d.). Kidshealth.org. https://kidshealth.org/en/teens/gratitude-practice.html

American Psychological Association. (2018). *Stress effects on the body*. American Psychological Association. https://www.apa.org/topics/stress/body

American Psychological Association. (2021). *Beyond worry: How psychologists help with anxiety disorders*. Apa.org. https://www.apa.org/topics/anxiety/disorders#:~:text =Anxiety%20disorders%20are%20very%20treatable

Andrews, A. F. (2020). *5 Times Billie Eilish got real about mental health*. Vogue. https://www.vogue.com/article/billie-eilish-march-cover-star-mental-health

Ankrom, S. (2021). *How to tell the difference of having a disorder or normal anxiety*. Verywell Mind. https://www.verywellmind.com/is-it-normal-anxiety-or-an-anxiety-disorder-2584401

Anxiety and Depression Association of America. (2021). *Facts & statistics*. Adaa.org; ADAA. https://adaa.org/understanding-anxiety/facts-statistics

Anxiety Canada. (n.d.). *Facing your fears: Exposure*. In Anxiety Canada. https://www.anxietycanada.com/sites/default/files/Fa cingFears_Exposure.pdf

Bethune, S. (2019). *Gen Z more likely to report mental health concerns.* Https://www.apa.org. https://www.apa.org/monitor/2019/01/gen-z

Better Health Channel. (2012). *Exercise and mental health.* Vic.gov.au. https://www.betterhealth.vic.gov.au/health/healthyliving/exercise-and-mental-health

Bieber, J. (2020). *Justin Bieber: Next chapter - A special documentary event (official).* Www.youtube.com. https://www.youtube.com/watch?v=RUcLuQ17UV8&feature=emb_title

Biswas, M. (2015). *Why you should start writing a thought diary.* Www.indusnet.co.in. https://www.indusnet.co.in/start-writing-thought-diary/

Blasberg, D. (2020). *The ballad of Selena Gomez.* Wall Street Journal. https://www.wsj.com/articles/selena-gomez-interview-cover-story-rare-11576604845

Bockarova, M. (2016). *4 Ways to set and keep your personal boundaries.* Psychology Today. https://www.psychologytoday.com/us/blog/romantically-attached/201608/4-ways-set-and-keep-your-personal-boundaries

Brenan, D. (2021). *Mental benefits of volunteering.* WebMD. https://www.webmd.com/mental-health/mental-benefits-of-volunteering#:~:text=Volunteers%20experience%20greater%20satisfaction%20with

Brightside Health. (2019). *9 Ways to improve your sleep to help with depression.* Brightside.

https://www.brightside.com/blog/9-ways-to-improve-your-sleep-to-help-with-depression/

Caplan, A. J. (2019). *How to start a new routine and stick to it.* Www.northshore.org. https://www.northshore.org/healthy-you/how-to-start-a-new-routine-and-stick-to-it/

CCI. (n.d.). *Helping health anxiety: Module 7 Challenging avoidance and safety behaviours.* Centre for Clinical Interventions. https://www.cci.health.wa.gov.au/~/media/CCI/Consumer-Modules/Helping-Health-Anxiety/Helping-Health-Anxiety---07---Challenging-Avoidance-and-Safety-Behaviours.pdf

Centre for Clinical Interventions. (n.d.). *Assert yourself! Module seven: How to deal assertively with criticism.* CCI. https://www.cci.health.wa.gov.au/-/media/CCI/Consumer-Modules/Assert-Yourself/Assert-Yourself---07----Dealing-With-Criticism-Assertively.pdf

Chand, S. (2019). *Social anxiety: Beware the silken trap of safety behaviors.* National Social Anxiety Center. https://nationalsocialanxietycenter.com/2019/11/23/social-anxiety-beware-the-silken-trap-of-safety-behaviors/

Cheeky Kid. (2022). *120+ Conversation starters for teens.* WeHaveKids. https://wehavekids.com/parenting/Conversation-Starters-for-Teens

Cohen, S. (1994). *Perceived stress scale.* In North Ottawa Wellness Foundation.

https://www.northottawawellnessfoundation.org/wp-content/uploads/2018/04/PerceivedStressScale.pdf

Collins, D. (2021). *Can listening to music reduce stress? Research, benefits, and genres.* Psych Central. https://psychcentral.com/stress/the-power-of-music-to-reduce-stress

Coppola, C. (2019). *Changing negative thoughts.* The Fantastic Life. https://thefantasticlife.com/changing-negative-thoughts/

Crichton-Stuart, C. (2018). *9 Foods that help reduce anxiety.* Www.medicalnewstoday.com. https://www.medicalnewstoday.com/articles/322652

Cuncic, A. (2020). *How to change your negative thought patterns when you have SAD.* Verywell Mind. https://www.verywellmind.com/how-to-change-negative-thinking-3024843

Fabrega, M. (2014). *8 Reasons why you need to spend more time in nature.* Daringtolivefully.com. https://daringtolivefully.com/spend-more-time-in-nature

Feller, S. (n.d.). *A guided meditation for self-love.* Yogainternational.com. https://yogainternational.com/article/view/guided-meditation-for-self-love

Firestone, L. (2010). *The critical inner voice that causes depression.* Www.psychologytoday.com. https://www.psychologytoday.com/za/blog/compassion-matters/201009/the-critical-inner-voice-causes-depression

For teens: Creating your personal stress management plan. (2019). HealthyChildren.org. https://www.healthychildren.org/English/healthy-living/emotional-wellness/Building-Resilience/Pages/For-Teens-Creating-Your-Personal-Stress-Management-Plan.aspx

Fox, L. (2020). *Demi Lovato admits she struggled with depression from the age of seven*. Mail Online. https://www.dailymail.co.uk/tvshowbiz/article-8722311/Demi-Lovato-admits-struggled-depression-suicidal-thoughts-age-seven.html

Fulghum Bruce, D. (2021). *Diet for depression* | Foods that help depression. WebMD. https://www.webmd.com/depression/guide/diet-recovery

Gupta, S. (2021). *What is exposure therapy?* Verywell Mind. https://www.verywellmind.com/exposure-therapy-definition-techniques-and-efficacy-5190514

Haskell, R. (2017). *Selena Gomez opens up about mental health and Instagram fatigue*. Vogue; Vogue. https://www.vogue.com/article/selena-gomez-april-cover-interview-mental-health-instagram

Healthwise Staff. (2018). *Stress management: Breathing exercises for relaxation*. Michigan Medicine. https://www.uofmhealth.org/health-library/uz2255

Heston, K. (2021). *How to do something new*. WikiHow. https://www.wikihow.com/Do-Something-New

Higuera, V. (2021). *Everything you want to know about depression*. Healthline.

https://www.healthline.com/health/depression#natura
l-remedies-and-lifestyle-tips

Holland, K. (2018). *20 Ways to fight depression*. Healthline.
https://www.healthline.com/health/depression/how-
to-fight-depression#step-back

Holland, K. (2020). *What triggers anxiety? 11 Causes that may
surprise you*. Healthline; Healthline Media.
https://www.healthline.com/health/anxiety/anxiety-
triggers

Jennings, K.-A., & Kubala, J. (2022). *16 Simple ways to relieve stress
and anxiety*. Healthline.
https://www.healthline.com/nutrition/16-ways-relieve-
stress-anxiety

Khorrami, N. (2020). *Gratitude helps curb anxiety*. Psychology
Today.
https://www.psychologytoday.com/za/blog/comfort-
gratitude/202007/gratitude-helps-curb-anxiety

Kovachis, S. (2017). *19 Self care ideas to take care of yourself*.
Canadian   Living.
https://www.canadianliving.com/health/mind-and-
spirit/article/19-simple-things-you-can-do-to-practice-
self-care

Lebowitz, S., & Watson, S. (2020). *26 Foods for your mood*.
Greatist.   https://greatist.com/happiness/25-meals-
boost-your-mood#breakfasts

Lorusso, M., & Barnes, S. (2019). *A look at mental health and
millennials*.   The   Millennial   Minds.
http://www.themillennialminds.com/

Mayo Clinic. (2018). *Depression (major depressive disorder)*. Mayo Clinic; Mayo Foundation for Medical Education and Research. https://www.mayoclinic.org/diseases-conditions/depression/symptoms-causes/syc-20356007

Mayo Clinic Staff. (2020). *6 Steps to better sleep*. Mayo Clinic. https://www.mayoclinic.org/healthy-lifestyle/adult-health/in-depth/sleep/art-20048379

McGee, K. R. (2020). *Is there a cure for anxiety?* GoodRx. https://www.goodrx.com/conditions/generalized-anxiety-disorder/cure

McNulty Counseling. (2021). *5 Tips to help set goals when you're depressed*. McNulty Counseling. https://www.mcnultycounseling.com/5-tips-to-help-set-goals-when-youre-depressed/

Mental Health America. (n.d.). How to keep a mental health journal. MHA Screening. https://screening.mhanational.org/content/how-keep-mental-health-journal/

Mental Health America. (2022). *The state of mental health in America*. Mhanational.org. https://www.mhanational.org/issues/state-mental-health-america

MentalHelp. (n.d.). *Building self-esteem by changing negative thoughts*. MentalHelp. https://www.mentalhelp.net/self-esteem/changing-negative-thoughts/

Mertins, B. (n.d.). *How to connect with nature*. Nature-Mentor.com. https://nature-mentor.com/how-to-connect-with-nature/

Mind. (2018). *How nature benefits mental health.* Www.mind.org.uk. https://www.mind.org.uk/information-support/tips-for-everyday-living/nature-and-mental-health/how-nature-benefits-mental-health/

Mindful Staff. (2019). *How to meditate.* Mindful. https://www.mindful.org/how-to-meditate/

Morin, A. (2018). *5 Simple parenting strategies that help kids build massive mental strength.* Incafrica.com. https://incafrica.com/library/amy-morin-5-simple-parenting-strategies-that-help-kids-build-massive-mental-strength

National Institute of Mental Health. (2019). *Anxiety disorders.* Nih.gov; National Institute of Mental Health. https://www.nimh.nih.gov/health/topics/anxiety-disorders

NHS. (2021a). *Treatment - Generalised anxiety disorder in adults.* Nhs.uk. https://www.nhs.uk/mental-health/conditions/generalised-anxiety-disorder/treatment/

NHS. (2021b). *Causes - Clinical depression.* Nhs.uk. https://www.nhs.uk/mental-health/conditions/clinical-depression/causes/

Paradigm Treatment. (2020). *Common causes of anxiety in teens and young adults.* Paradigm Treatment. https://paradigmtreatment.com/anxiety-teens-young-adults/common-causes/

Parekh, R. (2017). *What are anxiety disorders?* Psychiatry.org. https://www.psychiatry.org/patients-families/anxiety-disorders/what-are-anxiety-disorders

Psychologies. (2014). *How to wallow constructively.* Psychologies. https://www.psychologies.co.uk/how-to-wallow-constructively/

Rebecca. (2021). *10 Ways to spend quality time with someone.* Minimalism Made Simple. https://www.minimalismmadesimple.com/home/quality-time/

Scott, E. (2021). *Why avoidance coping creates additional stress.* Verywell Mind. https://www.verywellmind.com/avoidance-coping-and-stress-4137836

Shah, P. (2020). *7 Ways to help regulate your nervous system when stressed.* Chopra. https://chopra.com/articles/7-ways-to-help-regulate-your-nervous-system-when-stressed

Smith, E.-M. (2022). *What is negative thinking? How it destroys your mental health.* Www.healthyplace.com. https://www.healthyplace.com/self-help/positivity/what-is-negative-thinking-how-it-destroys-your-mental-health

Smith, K. (2016). *6 Common triggers of teen stress.* PsyCom.net - Mental Health Treatment Resource since 1986. https://www.psycom.net/common-triggers-teen-stress/

Smith, M., Robinson, L., & Segal, J. (2021a). *Coping with depression.* HelpGuide.org. https://www.helpguide.org/articles/depression/coping-with-depression.htm

Smith, M., Robinson, L., & Segal, J. (2021b). *Teenager's guide to depression.* HelpGuide.org.

https://www.helpguide.org/articles/depression/teenagers-guide-to-depression.htm

Spitzer, R. L. (n.d.). *GAD-7 (General Anxiety Disorder-7)*. MDCalc. https://www.mdcalc.com/gad-7-general-anxiety-disorder-7#why-use

Stanborough, R. J. (2019). *Cognitive distortions: 10 Examples of distorted thinking*. Healthline. https://www.healthline.com/health/cognitive-distortions#bottom-line

Sutton, J. (2021). *What is a thought diary in CBT? 5 Templates and examples*. PositivePsychology.com. https://positivepsychology.com/thought-diary/

Exposure: How to create a fear ladder step-by-step guide. (2020). The Regents of the University of Michigan. https://storage.trailstowellness.org/trails-2/resources/how-to-create-a-fear-ladder.pdf

Tomb, M. (2011). *IHC MHI Depression Fact Sheet: Children and Adolescents*. https://www.aacap.org/App_Themes/AACAP/docs/member_resources/toolbox_for_clinical_practice_and_outcomes/symptoms/GLAD-PC_PHQ-9.pdf

Torres, F. (2020). *What is depression?* Psychiatry; American Psychiatric Association. https://www.psychiatry.org/patients-families/depression/what-is-depression

Walters, J. (2011). *Why getting outside is so good for you*. SparkPeople. https://www.sparkpeople.com/resource/wellness_articles.asp?id=1680

Zoldan, R. J. (2022). *7 Beginner yoga poses to get through your first class.* Life by Daily Burn. https://dailyburn.com/life/fitness/beginner-yoga-poses-positions/

Image References

Cottonbro. (2021). Free stock photo of adolscent relaxing [Online image]. In Pexels. https://www.pexels.com/photo/dawn-love-woman-relaxation-6593737/

Grabowska, K. (2021). Young man in beige hoodie looking problematic while studying [Online image]. In Pexels. https://www.pexels.com/photo/young-man-in-beige-hoodie-looking-problematic-while-studying-6958533/

Green, A. (2020). Woman in desperate and anxiety sitting alone [Online image]. In Pexels. https://www.pexels.com/photo/woman-in-desperate-and-anxiety-sitting-alone-5699860/

Krukov, Y. (2021). A man pointing a pencil to a woman [Online image]. In Pexels. https://www.pexels.com/photo/a-man-pointing-a-pencil-to-a-woman-7640818/

Larson, J. (n.d.). Sporty trainer supporting black woman doing exercises with dumbbell [Online image]. In Pexels. https://www.pexels.com/photo/sporty-trainer-supporting-black-woman-doing-exercises-with-dumbbell-6455912/

Mart Production. (2021). Woman in white shirt sitting on bed [Online image]. In Pexels. https://www.pexels.com/photo/woman-in-white-shirt-sitting-on-bed-8472873/

Mentatdgt. (2018). Woman standing near man while carrying smartphone [Online image]. In Pexels. https://www.pexels.com/photo/woman-standing-near-man-while-carrying-smartphone-1186886/

Nilov, M. (2021a). Woman unrolling a yoga mat [Online image]. In Pexels. https://www.pexels.com/photo/woman-unrolling-a-yoga-mat-6740753/

Nilov, M. (2021b). Photo of a woman with her hands on her head [Online image]. In Pexels. https://www.pexels.com/photo/photo-of-a-woman-with-her-hands-on-her-head-8872807/

Piacquadio, A. (2020a). Exercising keeps oneself healthy [Online image]. In Pexels. https://www.pexels.com/photo/exercising-keeps-oneself-healthy-3768918/

Piacquadio, A. (2020b). Woman in red t-shirt looking at her laptop [Online image]. In Pexels. https://www.pexels.com/photo/woman-in-red-t-shirt-looking-at-her-laptop-3755761/

Piacquadio, A. (2020c). Woman in gray tank top while sitting on bed [Online image]. In Pexels. https://www.pexels.com/photo/woman-in-gray-tank-top-while-sitting-on-bed-3807730/

Piacquadio, A. (2020d). Exhausted mature man rubbing nose bridge after wearing glasses near gray wall [Online image]. In Pexels. https://www.pexels.com/photo/exhausted-mature-man-rubbing-nose-bridge-after-wearing-glasses-near-gray-wall-3974777/

Piacquadio, A. (2020e). Woman in green and white checkered dress shirt wearing brown framed eyeglasses [Online image]. In Pexels. https://www.pexels.com/photo/woman-in-green-and-white-checkered-dress-shirt-wearing-brown-framed-eyeglasses-3979152/

Shimazaki, S. (2020). Focused woman writing in clipboard while hiring candidate [Online image]. In Pexels. https://www.pexels.com/photo/focused-woman-writing-in-clipboard-while-hiring-candidate-5668869/

Shuraeva, A. (2020). Woman in white sweater thinking [Online image]. In Pexels. https://www.pexels.com/photo/woman-in-white-sweater-thinking-4091205/

SHVETS Production. (2021). Crop psychologist supporting patient during counseling indoors [Online image]. In Pexels. https://www.pexels.com/photo/crop-psychologist-supporting-patient-during-counseling-indoors-7176325/

Summer, L. (2021). Crop depressed black woman at home [Online image]. In Pexels. https://www.pexels.com/photo/crop-depressed-black-woman-at-home-6382661/

Made in the USA
Monee, IL
18 May 2022

96679807R00114